50 Caribbean Lunch Recipes for Home

By: Kelly Johnson

Table of Contents

- Jerk Chicken
- Curry Goat
- Rice and Peas
- Ackee and Saltfish
- Callaloo Soup
- Pepperpot
- Conch Fritters
- Roti
- Caribbean Fish Stew
- Coconut Shrimp
- Jamaican Beef Patty
- Trinidadian Doubles
- Barbadian Cou-Cou and Flying Fish
- Bahamian Crack Conch
- Grenadian Oil Down
- Haitian Griot
- Dominican Sancocho
- Cuban Ropa Vieja
- Stuffed Plantains
- Antiguan Pepperpot Soup
- St. Lucian Green Fig and Saltfish
- Cayman Islands Turtle Stew
- Jamaican Escovitch Fish
- Bajan Fish Cakes
- Puerto Rican Mofongo
- Guyanese Pepperpot
- Curry Chicken Roti
- Trini Pelau
- Dominican Mangu
- Haitian Joumou Soup
- St. Kitts and Nevis Goat Water
- Bahamian Conch Salad
- Jamaican Brown Stew Fish
- Curried Crab and Dumplings
- Barbadian Macaroni Pie
- Cuban Picadillo

- Trinidadian Callaloo and Crab
- Dominican Bandera Dominicana
- Jamaican Oxtail Stew
- Bahamian Chicken Souse
- Cuban Cubano Sandwich
- Puerto Rican Arroz con Gandules
- St. Lucian Breadfruit and Saltfish
- Grenadian Oil Down
- Haitian Legume
- Antiguan Ducana
- Guyanese Pepperpot
- Curry Goat and Roti
- St. Vincent and the Grenadines Roasted Breadfruit
- Bajan Cou-Cou

Jerk Chicken

Ingredients:

- 4-6 chicken thighs or drumsticks (bone-in, skin-on)
- 1/4 cup green onions (scallions), chopped
- 2-3 Scotch bonnet peppers (adjust to taste, or substitute with habanero peppers)
- 4 garlic cloves, minced
- 1 tablespoon fresh ginger, grated
- 2 tablespoons soy sauce
- 2 tablespoons vegetable oil
- 1 tablespoon brown sugar
- 1 tablespoon ground allspice
- 1 tablespoon dried thyme (or 2 tablespoons fresh thyme leaves)
- 1 teaspoon ground cinnamon
- 1 teaspoon ground nutmeg
- 1 teaspoon ground black pepper
- 1 teaspoon salt
- Juice of 1 lime
- Juice of 1 orange
- 1/4 cup vinegar (apple cider vinegar or white vinegar)
- Optional: 1 tablespoon rum (dark or spiced)

Instructions:

1. **Prepare the Marinade:**
   - In a food processor or blender, combine the green onions, Scotch bonnet peppers, garlic, ginger, soy sauce, vegetable oil, brown sugar, allspice, thyme, cinnamon, nutmeg, black pepper, salt, lime juice, orange juice, vinegar, and rum (if using). Blend until smooth.
2. **Marinate the Chicken:**
   - Place the chicken pieces in a large bowl or resealable plastic bag. Pour the marinade over the chicken, making sure each piece is well coated. Seal the bag or cover the bowl with plastic wrap. Refrigerate and marinate for at least 4 hours, preferably overnight for best flavor.
3. **Preheat the Grill:**
   - Preheat your grill to medium-high heat (about 375-400°F / 190-200°C). Brush the grill grates lightly with oil to prevent sticking.
4. **Grill the Chicken:**
   - Remove the chicken from the marinade, letting any excess drip off. Reserve the marinade for basting.
   - Place the chicken pieces on the grill, skin-side down. Grill for about 6-8 minutes per side, basting occasionally with the reserved marinade, until the chicken is cooked through and has nice grill marks. The internal temperature should reach 165°F (75°C).

5. **Rest and Serve:**
    - Once cooked, transfer the jerk chicken to a serving platter and let it rest for a few minutes before serving.
    - Serve hot with traditional sides like rice and peas, grilled vegetables, or coleslaw.

Enjoy your homemade Jerk Chicken with its bold flavors and spicy kick, typical of Caribbean cuisine! Adjust the heat level by varying the amount of Scotch bonnet peppers to suit your taste preferences.

Rice and Peas

Ingredients:

- 1 cup long grain white rice (preferably jasmine or basmati)
- 1 cup canned kidney beans (or 1 1/2 cups cooked kidney beans)
- 1 1/2 cups coconut milk
- 1 cup water
- 2-3 cloves garlic, minced
- 2-3 green onions (scallions), chopped
- 1 small onion, finely chopped
- 1 sprig fresh thyme (or 1 teaspoon dried thyme)
- 1/2 teaspoon ground allspice
- Salt and pepper, to taste
- Scotch bonnet pepper or hot sauce (optional, for heat)
- 1 tablespoon vegetable oil

Instructions:

1. **Prepare the Beans:**
    - If using canned kidney beans, rinse and drain them thoroughly. If using dried beans, soak them overnight in water, then cook until tender before using.
2. **Cooking the Rice and Peas:**
    - In a large pot or Dutch oven, heat the vegetable oil over medium heat. Add the chopped onions, garlic, and green onions. Sauté for 2-3 minutes until softened and fragrant.
3. **Add Coconut Milk and Seasonings:**
    - Stir in the coconut milk, water, thyme, allspice, salt, and pepper. Bring the mixture to a simmer.
4. **Add Rice and Beans:**
    - Add the rice and kidney beans to the pot, stirring well to combine. If using Scotch bonnet pepper, you can add it whole (for mild heat) or chopped (for more heat) at this stage.
5. **Simmer:**
    - Reduce the heat to low, cover the pot with a lid, and let it simmer gently for 20-25 minutes, or until the rice is cooked and most of the liquid is absorbed. Stir occasionally to prevent sticking.
6. **Fluff and Serve:**
    - Once the rice is cooked, remove the pot from the heat. Fluff the rice and peas with a fork to mix everything evenly. Taste and adjust seasoning if needed.
7. **Serve:**
    - Serve the Rice and Peas hot as a side dish with your favorite Caribbean main dishes such as Jerk Chicken, Curry Goat, or Fried Fish.

Enjoy this comforting and flavorful Rice and Peas dish, which brings together the richness of coconut milk with the earthy flavors of beans and aromatic spices, typical of Caribbean cooking!

Callaloo Soup

Ingredients:

- 1 bunch of callaloo leaves (about 1 lb), washed and chopped (substitute with spinach or Swiss chard if callaloo leaves are not available)
- 1 onion, finely chopped
- 2 cloves garlic, minced
- 1 medium tomato, chopped
- 1 small carrot, diced
- 1 medium potato, peeled and diced
- 4 cups vegetable or chicken broth
- 1 cup coconut milk
- 1 tablespoon olive oil or vegetable oil
- 1/2 teaspoon ground allspice
- 1/2 teaspoon dried thyme (or 1 sprig fresh thyme)
- Salt and pepper, to taste
- Scotch bonnet pepper or hot sauce (optional, for heat)
- Juice of 1 lime or lemon (optional, for a tangy flavor)

Instructions:

1. **Prepare the Callaloo Leaves:**
   - Wash the callaloo leaves thoroughly to remove any dirt or grit. Remove tough stems and chop the leaves finely.
2. **Sauté Aromatics:**
   - In a large pot or Dutch oven, heat the olive oil over medium heat. Add the chopped onion and garlic. Sauté for 2-3 minutes until the onions are translucent and fragrant.
3. **Add Vegetables:**
   - Add the chopped tomato, diced carrot, and diced potato to the pot. Stir and cook for another 3-4 minutes.
4. **Add Broth and Seasonings:**
   - Pour in the vegetable or chicken broth. Add the allspice, dried thyme (or fresh thyme sprig), salt, and pepper. If using Scotch bonnet pepper or hot sauce, add it now according to your spice preference.
5. **Simmer:**
   - Bring the soup to a boil, then reduce the heat to low. Cover the pot and simmer for about 15-20 minutes, or until the vegetables are tender.
6. **Blend or Mash:**
   - Once the vegetables are cooked, use an immersion blender to blend the soup until smooth. Alternatively, you can transfer portions of the soup to a blender and blend until smooth, then return it to the pot.
7. **Add Coconut Milk:**

- Stir in the coconut milk and simmer for another 5 minutes to heat through and allow the flavors to meld together.
8. **Adjust Seasoning and Serve:**
    - Taste the soup and adjust seasoning if needed, adding more salt, pepper, or lime/lemon juice for extra flavor.
9. **Serve:**
    - Ladle the Callaloo Soup into bowls. Garnish with a drizzle of coconut milk or a sprig of fresh thyme if desired. Serve hot with crusty bread or fried plantains.

Enjoy this creamy and flavorful Callaloo Soup, which is rich in Caribbean flavors and perfect for a comforting meal!

Curry Goat

Ingredients:

- 2 lbs goat meat, cut into chunks (preferably bone-in for more flavor)
- 2 tablespoons curry powder
- 1 onion, chopped
- 4 cloves garlic, minced
- 1 tablespoon fresh ginger, grated
- 2 tomatoes, chopped
- 2 tablespoons vegetable oil
- 1 tablespoon tomato paste
- 1 teaspoon ground allspice
- 1 teaspoon ground cumin
- 1 teaspoon ground turmeric
- 1 teaspoon ground coriander
- 1/2 teaspoon ground cinnamon
- 2 cups beef or vegetable broth
- 1 cup coconut milk
- 2-3 sprigs fresh thyme (or 1 teaspoon dried thyme)
- Salt and pepper, to taste
- Scotch bonnet pepper or hot sauce (optional, for heat)
- Juice of 1 lime or lemon

Instructions:

1. **Marinate the Goat Meat:**
   - In a large bowl, season the goat meat with the curry powder, salt, and pepper. Massage the spices into the meat, ensuring each piece is coated. Let it marinate for at least 30 minutes, or ideally overnight in the refrigerator for deeper flavor.
2. **Sear the Meat:**
   - In a large Dutch oven or heavy-bottomed pot, heat the vegetable oil over medium-high heat. Add the marinated goat meat in batches, searing each side until browned. Remove the meat and set aside.
3. **Sauté Aromatics:**
   - In the same pot, add the chopped onion, garlic, and grated ginger. Sauté for 2-3 minutes until the onions are translucent and fragrant.
4. **Add Spices and Tomatoes:**
   - Stir in the ground allspice, cumin, turmeric, coriander, cinnamon, and tomato paste. Cook for another minute to toast the spices.
   - Add the chopped tomatoes and cook for 3-4 minutes until they start to break down.
5. **Simmer the Curry:**

- Return the seared goat meat to the pot. Pour in the beef or vegetable broth and coconut milk. Add the fresh thyme sprigs (or dried thyme). If using Scotch bonnet pepper or hot sauce for heat, add it now.
- Bring the mixture to a boil, then reduce the heat to low. Cover the pot and simmer for 1.5 to 2 hours, or until the goat meat is tender and falls off the bone. Stir occasionally and add more broth or water if needed to keep the meat covered.

6. **Finish and Serve:**
   - Taste the curry and adjust seasoning with salt, pepper, and lime or lemon juice as needed.
   - Serve hot over rice and peas, with roti, or with your favorite Caribbean side dishes.

Enjoy this hearty and aromatic Curry Goat, which combines tender goat meat with a fragrant curry sauce that's perfect for warming up any mealtime with Caribbean flavors!

Ackee and Saltfish

Ingredients:

- 1 lb salted codfish (saltfish)
- 1 can (19 oz) ackee, drained and rinsed (fresh ackee can also be used if available)
- 1 onion, finely chopped
- 1 bell pepper (red or green), chopped
- 2 cloves garlic, minced
- 2 tomatoes, chopped
- 2 tablespoons vegetable oil
- 1/2 teaspoon ground black pepper
- Scotch bonnet pepper or hot sauce (optional, for heat)
- Fresh thyme leaves (optional)
- Salt (if needed, depending on saltiness of the saltfish)
- Green onions (scallions), chopped (for garnish)
- Serve with boiled green bananas, dumplings, fried plantains, or bread (optional)

Instructions:

1. **Prepare the Saltfish:**
   - Rinse the saltfish under cold water to remove excess salt. Place it in a bowl and cover with cold water. Let it soak for at least 1 hour, or overnight in the refrigerator, changing the water a few times to desalinate. After soaking, drain and rinse again.
2. **Cook the Saltfish:**
   - In a pot, cover the soaked saltfish with water and bring to a boil. Simmer for about 10-15 minutes, or until the fish flakes easily with a fork. Drain the fish and let it cool slightly. Remove any bones and flake the fish into small pieces.
3. **Sauté Aromatics:**
   - In a large skillet or frying pan, heat the vegetable oil over medium heat. Add the chopped onion, bell pepper, and minced garlic. Sauté for 3-4 minutes until the vegetables are softened and fragrant.
4. **Add Tomatoes and Seasonings:**
   - Add the chopped tomatoes to the skillet and cook for another 2-3 minutes until they start to break down. Stir in the ground black pepper and fresh thyme leaves (if using). If using Scotch bonnet pepper or hot sauce for heat, add it now according to your preference.
5. **Combine Ackee and Saltfish:**
   - Gently fold in the flaked saltfish and drained ackee into the skillet with the sautéed vegetables. Be careful not to stir too vigorously to avoid breaking up the ackee.
6. **Cook Together:**
   - Cook the mixture over low heat for 5-7 minutes, stirring gently occasionally, until the ackee is heated through and well combined with the saltfish and vegetables.

7. **Adjust Seasoning and Serve:**
    - Taste and adjust seasoning with salt and pepper if needed (be cautious with salt as the saltfish may already be salty).
    - Serve hot, garnished with chopped green onions (scallions), alongside boiled green bananas, dumplings, fried plantains, or bread.

Enjoy this flavorful and hearty Jamaican dish of Ackee and Saltfish, perfect for any meal of the day!

Roti

Ingredients:

- 3 cups all-purpose flour
- 1 teaspoon salt
- 1 tablespoon baking powder
- 1 cup warm water
- 1/4 cup vegetable oil or melted butter

Instructions:

1. **Prepare the Dough:**
   - In a large mixing bowl, combine the flour, salt, and baking powder. Mix well.
   - Gradually add the warm water, a little at a time, while mixing with your hands or a wooden spoon, until the dough starts to come together.
2. **Knead the Dough:**
   - Transfer the dough onto a lightly floured surface and knead for about 8-10 minutes until it becomes smooth and elastic. If the dough is too sticky, add a little more flour; if it's too dry, add a little more water.
3. **Rest the Dough:**
   - Shape the dough into a smooth ball and coat it lightly with vegetable oil. Place it back in the mixing bowl and cover with a clean kitchen towel or plastic wrap. Let it rest at room temperature for at least 30 minutes (up to 2 hours) to allow the gluten to relax.
4. **Divide and Shape the Dough:**
   - After resting, divide the dough into 8 equal portions. Roll each portion into a ball.
5. **Roll Out the Roti:**
   - On a lightly floured surface, roll out each ball of dough into a thin, round circle (about 6-8 inches in diameter) using a rolling pin. Aim for even thickness.
6. **Cook the Roti:**
   - Heat a griddle or large non-stick skillet over medium-high heat. Place a rolled-out roti onto the hot griddle and cook for about 1-2 minutes on each side, or until small bubbles start to form and the underside has brown spots.
7. **Finish Cooking:**
   - Brush the cooked roti with a little vegetable oil or melted butter on both sides while it's still hot. This helps keep the roti soft and adds flavor.
8. **Serve:**
   - Stack the cooked roti on a plate and cover with a clean kitchen towel to keep them warm and soft.
   - Serve the roti warm with your favorite curry or filling. Popular fillings include curried vegetables, chickpeas, or meats such as chicken or goat.

Enjoy your homemade Trinidadian Roti, a delicious and versatile flatbread that complements a wide range of Caribbean dishes!

Fried Plantains

Ingredients:

- 2 ripe plantains (yellow with some black spots)
- Vegetable oil, for frying
- Salt (optional)

Instructions:

1. **Prepare the Plantains:**
    - Choose ripe plantains that are yellow with some black spots on the peel. Peel the plantains by cutting off the ends and making a slit along the length of each plantain. Remove the peel and discard.
2. **Slice the Plantains:**
    - Cut the peeled plantains into diagonal slices, about 1/2 inch thick. You can also cut them into rounds if you prefer.
3. **Heat the Oil:**
    - In a large skillet or frying pan, heat enough vegetable oil to cover the bottom of the pan over medium heat. The oil should be hot but not smoking.
4. **Fry the Plantains:**
    - Carefully place the plantain slices in the hot oil, making sure not to overcrowd the pan. Fry for about 2-3 minutes on each side, or until golden brown and caramelized.
5. **Drain and Serve:**
    - Remove the fried plantains from the oil using a slotted spoon or tongs, and place them on a plate lined with paper towels to drain excess oil.
6. **Season (optional):**
    - Sprinkle the fried plantains with a pinch of salt while they are still hot, if desired. This enhances the flavor.
7. **Serve:**
    - Serve the fried plantains warm as a side dish or snack. They pair well with rice and beans, grilled meats, or as a delicious treat on their own.

Enjoy your crispy and sweet fried plantains, a delightful taste of the Caribbean! Adjust the cooking time slightly depending on how ripe the plantains are and your desired level of caramelization.

Jamaican Patties

Ingredients:

For the Pastry Dough:

- 2 cups all-purpose flour
- 1/2 teaspoon salt
- 1/2 cup cold unsalted butter, cut into small cubes
- 1/2 cup cold water

For the Meat Filling:

- 1 lb ground beef (you can also use ground chicken, turkey, or a mixture)
- 1 onion, finely chopped
- 2 cloves garlic, minced
- 1 small potato, peeled and finely diced (optional, for texture)
- 1/2 cup frozen mixed vegetables (peas and carrots)
- 2 tablespoons curry powder
- 1 teaspoon turmeric powder
- 1/2 teaspoon thyme (dried or fresh)
- 1/2 teaspoon paprika
- 1/4 teaspoon cayenne pepper (optional, for heat)
- Salt and pepper, to taste
- 1/2 cup beef or chicken broth
- Vegetable oil, for cooking

Instructions:

1. **Make the Pastry Dough:**
   - In a large bowl, whisk together the flour and salt. Add the cold butter cubes and rub them into the flour using your fingertips until the mixture resembles coarse breadcrumbs.
   - Gradually add the cold water, a little at a time, and mix until the dough comes together. You may not need to use all the water. Form the dough into a ball, wrap it in plastic wrap, and refrigerate for at least 30 minutes.
2. **Prepare the Meat Filling:**
   - Heat a tablespoon of vegetable oil in a large skillet over medium heat. Add the chopped onion and garlic, and sauté until softened and translucent.
   - Add the ground beef to the skillet and cook until browned, breaking it up with a spoon as it cooks.
   - Stir in the diced potato (if using), frozen mixed vegetables, curry powder, turmeric powder, thyme, paprika, cayenne pepper (if using), salt, and pepper. Cook for another 2-3 minutes, stirring frequently.

- Pour in the beef or chicken broth and simmer until the liquid has reduced and the filling is thickened. Remove from heat and let the filling cool completely.
3. **Assemble the Patties:**
    - Preheat your oven to 375°F (190°C) and line a baking sheet with parchment paper.
    - On a lightly floured surface, roll out the chilled pastry dough to about 1/8 inch thickness. Use a round cutter (about 5-6 inches in diameter) to cut out circles of dough.
4. **Fill and Seal the Patties:**
    - Place a spoonful of the cooled meat filling onto one half of each dough circle, leaving a small border around the edges.
    - Fold the other half of the dough over the filling to form a half-moon shape. Press the edges together firmly to seal.
    - Use a fork to crimp the edges of each patty to ensure they are securely sealed.
5. **Bake the Patties:**
    - Arrange the sealed patties on the prepared baking sheet. Brush the tops lightly with beaten egg or milk for a golden finish (optional).
    - Bake in the preheated oven for 25-30 minutes, or until the patties are golden brown and crispy.
6. **Serve:**
    - Remove the patties from the oven and let them cool slightly before serving.
    - Enjoy your homemade Jamaican Patties warm or at room temperature as a delicious snack or meal!

These Jamaican Patties are filled with flavorful spiced meat and encased in a flaky pastry crust, perfect for sharing with friends and family or enjoying as a tasty treat on the go.

Conch Fritters

Ingredients:

- 1 lb conch meat, cleaned and finely chopped (you can also use pre-cooked conch meat)
- 1 cup all-purpose flour
- 1/2 cup cornmeal
- 1/2 teaspoon baking powder
- 1/2 teaspoon salt
- 1/4 teaspoon black pepper
- 1/4 teaspoon cayenne pepper (optional, for heat)
- 1/2 cup finely chopped bell pepper (red, green, or both)
- 1/2 cup finely chopped onion
- 1/4 cup finely chopped celery
- 2 cloves garlic, minced
- 2 tablespoons fresh parsley, chopped
- 1 tablespoon fresh thyme leaves (or 1 teaspoon dried thyme)
- 1/2 cup milk
- 1 large egg, beaten
- Vegetable oil, for frying
- Lime wedges, for serving
- Cocktail sauce or tartar sauce, for dipping (optional)

Instructions:

1. **Prepare the Conch:**
    - If using fresh conch meat, clean and finely chop it. If using pre-cooked conch meat, ensure it is finely chopped.
2. **Make the Batter:**
    - In a large bowl, combine the flour, cornmeal, baking powder, salt, black pepper, and cayenne pepper (if using).
    - Add the chopped bell pepper, onion, celery, garlic, parsley, and thyme to the dry ingredients. Mix well to combine.
3. **Mix in Wet Ingredients:**
    - In a separate bowl, whisk together the milk and beaten egg.
    - Gradually add the milk and egg mixture to the dry ingredients, stirring until a thick batter forms. The batter should be thick enough to hold its shape when spooned.
4. **Add Conch Meat:**
    - Fold the chopped conch meat into the batter, ensuring it is evenly distributed.
5. **Fry the Fritters:**
    - Heat vegetable oil in a deep skillet or frying pan over medium-high heat until it reaches 350°F (175°C).
    - Drop spoonfuls of the conch batter into the hot oil, using a tablespoon or small ice cream scoop. Be careful not to overcrowd the pan.

- Fry the fritters for about 3-4 minutes, turning occasionally, until they are golden brown and crispy on all sides.

6. **Drain and Serve:**
    - Remove the fritters from the oil using a slotted spoon and drain on a plate lined with paper towels to absorb excess oil.
    - Serve the conch fritters hot, garnished with fresh parsley and lime wedges on the side.
    - Optional: Serve with cocktail sauce or tartar sauce for dipping.

Enjoy these crispy and flavorful conch fritters as a delicious appetizer or snack, bringing a taste of the Caribbean to your table!

Pepperpot

Ingredients:

- 2 lbs beef (bone-in), cubed
- 1 lb pork (bone-in), cubed
- 1 lb oxtails (optional), cut into pieces
- 1/2 lb cow heel (optional), cut into pieces
- 1/2 lb salted pigtail or salted beef, cut into pieces
- 2 cups cassareep (available in Caribbean or specialty stores)
- 4-6 cups water (enough to cover the meats)
- 1 onion, chopped
- 4 cloves garlic, minced
- 2-3 wiri wiri peppers or Scotch bonnet peppers, whole (adjust to taste)
- 1 cinnamon stick
- 4 cloves
- 4 bay leaves
- Salt and pepper, to taste
- Vegetable oil, for frying

Instructions:

1. **Prepare the Meats:**
   - Rinse the salted meats (salted pigtail or salted beef) under cold water to remove excess salt. Place them in a large pot or bowl with cold water and let soak for 1-2 hours, changing the water a few times.
2. **Brown the Meats (optional):**
   - In a large Dutch oven or heavy-bottomed pot, heat a little vegetable oil over medium-high heat. Brown the cubed beef, pork, oxtails, and cow heel pieces in batches until they are nicely browned on all sides. Remove and set aside.
3. **Cook the Aromatics:**
   - In the same pot, add a bit more oil if needed and sauté the chopped onion and minced garlic until softened and fragrant.
4. **Combine and Simmer:**
   - Return all the browned meats to the pot. Add enough water to cover the meats (about 4-6 cups).
   - Stir in the cassareep until well combined. Add the wiri wiri peppers or Scotch bonnet peppers (whole for less heat, sliced for more heat), cinnamon stick, cloves, and bay leaves. Season with salt and pepper to taste.
5. **Simmer the Pepperpot:**
   - Bring the mixture to a boil, then reduce the heat to low. Cover the pot and simmer gently for 2-3 hours, stirring occasionally, until the meats are tender and the sauce has thickened. Add more water if needed to achieve your desired consistency.
6. **Serve:**

- Remove the wiri wiri peppers or Scotch bonnet peppers, cinnamon stick, cloves, and bay leaves before serving.
- Pepperpot is traditionally served hot with rice, roti, or bread.

Enjoy the rich and hearty flavors of Pepperpot, a dish that reflects the culinary diversity and traditions of the Caribbean region, especially during festive occasions! Adjust the spice level by controlling the amount of wiri wiri or Scotch bonnet peppers used.

Doubles (Trinidadian street food)

Ingredients:

For the Bara (Fried Flatbread):

- 2 cups all-purpose flour
- 1 teaspoon baking powder
- 1/2 teaspoon ground turmeric (optional,

for color)

- 1/2 teaspoon salt
- 1/2 teaspoon ground cumin
- 1/4 teaspoon ground black pepper
- 1/2 teaspoon yeast
- 1/2 cup warm water
- Vegetable oil, for frying

For the Channa (Chickpea Curry):

- 1 cup dried chickpeas (or 2 cans chickpeas, drained and rinsed)
- 2 tablespoons vegetable oil
- 1 onion, finely chopped
- 3 cloves garlic, minced
- 1 tablespoon curry powder
- 1/2 teaspoon ground cumin
- 1/2 teaspoon ground turmeric
- 1/4 teaspoon cayenne pepper (adjust to taste)
- 1 cup water (if using dried chickpeas)
- Salt and pepper, to taste
- 1 tablespoon chopped fresh cilantro (optional, for garnish)

Optional Toppings:

- Tamarind sauce or tamarind chutney
- Cucumber chutney or salsa
- Shredded lettuce or cabbage
- Hot pepper sauce or chopped hot peppers

Instructions:

For the Bara (Fried Flatbread):

1. **Prepare the Dough:**

- In a large bowl, combine the flour, baking powder, turmeric (if using), salt, cumin, and black pepper.
- In a small bowl, dissolve the yeast in warm water and let it sit for 5 minutes until frothy.
- Make a well in the center of the dry ingredients and pour in the yeast mixture.

2. **Mix and Knead:**
   - Gradually incorporate the flour into the liquid, mixing until a soft dough forms.
   - Turn the dough out onto a lightly floured surface and knead for about 5-7 minutes until smooth and elastic.
   - Place the dough in a bowl greased with oil, cover with a damp cloth, and let it rest in a warm place for 1-2 hours, or until doubled in size.

3. **Shape and Fry the Bara:**
   - Divide the dough into 8-10 equal portions. Roll each portion into a ball, then flatten with your hands or a rolling pin to form rounds about 5-6 inches in diameter.
   - Heat vegetable oil in a deep frying pan or skillet over medium heat.
   - Fry the bara, one at a time, in hot oil until golden brown and puffed up, about 1-2 minutes on each side. Drain on paper towels and keep warm.

For the Channa (Chickpea Curry):

1. **Prepare the Chickpeas (if using dried):**
   - If using dried chickpeas, soak them overnight in water. Drain and rinse the chickpeas.
   - In a large pot, cover the chickpeas with fresh water and

bring to a boil. Reduce heat and simmer for about 1 hour, or until tender. Drain and set aside.

2. **Cook the Channa Curry:**
   - In a large skillet or saucepan, heat vegetable oil over medium heat. Add the chopped onion and sauté until translucent, about 3-4 minutes.
   - Add the minced garlic, curry powder, ground cumin, ground turmeric, and cayenne pepper. Cook, stirring constantly, for another 1-2 minutes until fragrant.
   - Stir in the cooked chickpeas (or canned chickpeas, drained and rinsed). Add 1 cup of water (or more as needed to achieve desired consistency).
   - Season with salt and pepper to taste. Simmer the mixture for 10-15 minutes, stirring occasionally, until the flavors meld and the curry thickens slightly.
   - Remove from heat and stir in chopped fresh cilantro, if using.

Assembly:

1. **Serve Doubles:**
   - To assemble doubles, place a piece of bara on a plate. Spoon a generous amount of channa curry onto the bara.

        - Top with optional toppings such as tamarind sauce, cucumber chutney, shredded lettuce, and hot pepper sauce.
        - Optionally, fold the bara over the filling like a sandwich or place another piece of bara on top to create a "double."
  2. **Enjoy:**
        - Serve doubles immediately while warm. They are best enjoyed as a handheld street food or snack, perfect for sharing and enjoying the flavors of Trinidad and Tobago.

Doubles are a delicious and satisfying dish that captures the essence of Trinidadian street food culture. The combination of soft, fried bara with spicy channa curry and various toppings creates a flavorful and memorable culinary experience.

Bajan Fish Fry

Ingredients:

- 2 lbs fresh fish fillets (such as snapper, mahi-mahi, or any firm white fish)
- 1 cup all-purpose flour
- 1 teaspoon salt
- 1/2 teaspoon black pepper
- 1/2 teaspoon paprika
- 1/4 teaspoon cayenne pepper (adjust to taste)
- Vegetable oil, for frying
- Lime or lemon wedges, for serving
- Fresh parsley or cilantro, chopped (for garnish)

Instructions:

1. **Prepare the Fish:**
    - Rinse the fish fillets under cold water and pat dry with paper towels. Cut the fillets into smaller pieces, if desired, for easier frying.
2. **Season the Flour:**
    - In a shallow dish or bowl, combine the flour, salt, black pepper, paprika, and cayenne pepper. Mix well to combine the seasonings evenly.
3. **Coat the Fish:**
    - Heat vegetable oil in a large skillet or frying pan over medium-high heat, enough to cover the bottom of the pan generously.
    - Dredge each piece of fish in the seasoned flour mixture, shaking off any excess flour.
4. **Fry the Fish:**
    - Carefully place the coated fish fillets into the hot oil, working in batches if necessary to avoid overcrowding the pan.
    - Fry the fish for about 3-4 minutes on each side, or until golden brown and crispy. Adjust the heat as needed to maintain a steady frying temperature.
5. **Drain and Serve:**
    - Remove the fried fish from the oil using a slotted spoon or spatula, and place them on a plate lined with paper towels to drain excess oil.
    - Serve the Bajan fish fry hot, garnished with chopped fresh parsley or cilantro and accompanied by lime or lemon wedges for squeezing over the fish.
6. **Serving Suggestions:**
    - Bajan fish fry is traditionally served with sides such as coleslaw, fried plantains, macaroni pie, or rice and peas. It pairs wonderfully with a cold beverage or a local Bajan rum punch!

Enjoy this Bajan Fish Fry recipe, capturing the flavors of Barbados with crispy fried fish that's perfect for a satisfying meal with a taste of the Caribbean.

Caribbean Chicken Curry

Ingredients:

- 2 lbs chicken thighs or breasts, boneless and skinless, cut into bite-sized pieces
- 2 tablespoons curry powder
- 1 teaspoon ground turmeric
- 1 teaspoon ground cumin
- 1/2 teaspoon ground coriander
- 1/4 teaspoon cayenne pepper (adjust to taste)
- Salt and pepper, to taste
- 2 tablespoons vegetable oil or coconut oil
- 1 onion, finely chopped
- 3 cloves garlic, minced
- 1-inch piece of ginger, grated or minced
- 1 bell pepper, chopped (red, green, or yellow)
- 1 medium potato, peeled and diced
- 1 carrot, diced
- 1 cup coconut milk
- 1 cup chicken broth or water
- 2 tablespoons tomato paste
- Fresh cilantro, chopped, for garnish
- Cooked rice or roti, for serving

Instructions:

1. **Prepare the Chicken:**
   - In a bowl, combine the chicken pieces with curry powder, turmeric, cumin, coriander, cayenne pepper, salt, and pepper. Mix well to coat the chicken evenly with the spices. Let it marinate for at least 15-20 minutes, or refrigerate for up to 2 hours for more flavor.
2. **Sear the Chicken:**
   - Heat vegetable oil or coconut oil in a large skillet or Dutch oven over medium-high heat. Add the marinated chicken pieces in batches and sear until browned on all sides. Remove the chicken from the skillet and set aside.
3. **Cook the Aromatics:**
   - In the same skillet or Dutch oven, add a bit more oil if needed. Sauté the chopped onion, garlic, and grated ginger until softened and fragrant, about 3-4 minutes.
4. **Add Vegetables and Spices:**
   - Add the chopped bell pepper, diced potato, and carrot to the skillet. Cook for another 5 minutes, stirring occasionally, until the vegetables begin to soften.
   - Stir in the tomato paste and cook for 1-2 minutes to deepen the flavor.
5. **Simmer the Curry:**

- Return the seared chicken pieces to the skillet. Pour in the coconut milk and chicken broth (or water). Stir well to combine all ingredients.
- Bring the mixture to a simmer. Reduce the heat to low, cover, and let it simmer gently for 20-25 minutes, or until the chicken is cooked through and the vegetables are tender. Stir occasionally.

6. **Adjust Seasoning and Serve:**
   - Taste the curry and adjust seasoning with salt and pepper if needed. If you prefer a thicker curry, you can simmer uncovered for a few more minutes to reduce the liquid.
   - Garnish the Caribbean Chicken Curry with chopped fresh cilantro before serving.
   - Serve hot over cooked rice or with roti, naan, or bread of your choice.

Enjoy this delicious Caribbean Chicken Curry, rich with spices and flavors that are characteristic of Caribbean cuisine. It's perfect for a comforting and satisfying meal that will transport you to the islands!

Stewed Oxtail

Ingredients:

- 3-4 lbs oxtail, cut into segments
- Salt and pepper, to taste
- 2 tablespoons vegetable oil
- 1 large onion, chopped
- 4 cloves garlic, minced
- 2 stalks celery, chopped
- 2 carrots, peeled and sliced
- 2 bay leaves
- 1 teaspoon dried thyme (or 2-3 sprigs fresh thyme)
- 1 tablespoon tomato paste
- 2 cups beef broth or water
- 1 cup red wine (optional)
- 1 tablespoon Worcestershire sauce
- 2 tablespoons soy sauce
- 1 tablespoon brown sugar (optional, for sweetness)
- 2-3 cups water, as needed
- Chopped fresh parsley or cilantro, for garnish

Instructions:

1. **Prepare the Oxtail:**
   - Rinse the oxtail pieces under cold water and pat dry with paper towels. Season generously with salt and pepper.
2. **Brown the Oxtail:**
   - Heat vegetable oil in a large Dutch oven or heavy-bottomed pot over medium-high heat. Brown the oxtail pieces on all sides, working in batches if necessary to avoid overcrowding the pot. This step helps develop flavor through caramelization. Remove the browned oxtail and set aside.
3. **Sauté Aromatics:**
   - In the same pot, add chopped onion, minced garlic, celery, and carrots. Sauté for about 5 minutes until the vegetables begin to soften.
4. **Add Seasonings and Liquids:**
   - Stir in bay leaves, dried thyme (or fresh thyme), and tomato paste. Cook for another 1-2 minutes to toast the tomato paste slightly.
   - Deglaze the pot by pouring in beef broth (or water) and red wine (if using), scraping up any browned bits from the bottom of the pot.
   - Add Worcestershire sauce, soy sauce, and brown sugar (if using) to enhance the flavors. Stir to combine.
5. **Simmer the Oxtail:**
   - Return the browned oxtail pieces to the pot, along with any juices that have accumulated. Add enough water to cover the oxtail (about 2-3 cups).

- Bring the mixture to a boil, then reduce the heat to low. Cover the pot and let it simmer gently for 3-4 hours, or until the oxtail is tender and falling off the bone. Stir occasionally and add more water if needed to keep the oxtail covered during cooking.

6. **Finish and Serve:**
   - Once the oxtail is tender, taste and adjust seasoning with salt and pepper if necessary.
   - Serve the stewed oxtail hot, garnished with chopped fresh parsley or cilantro.
   - Enjoy this hearty and flavorful Caribbean stewed oxtail with rice, mashed potatoes, or your favorite side dish.

Stewed oxtail is a comforting dish that showcases the rich and delicious flavors of Caribbean cuisine. It's perfect for special occasions or any time you want a hearty and satisfying meal!

Fish Escovitch

Ingredients:

- 2 whole fish (such as snapper, tilapia, or any firm white fish), cleaned and scaled
- Salt and pepper, to taste
- Vegetable oil, for frying

For the Escovitch Sauce:

- 1 large onion, thinly sliced
- 1 bell pepper (red or yellow), thinly sliced
- 1 carrot, julienned or thinly sliced
- 2 Scotch bonnet peppers (or habanero peppers), thinly sliced
- 1 cup white vinegar
- 1/4 cup water
- 2 tablespoons sugar
- 1 teaspoon salt
- 1 teaspoon whole allspice berries
- 1/2 teaspoon ground black pepper
- 3-4 sprigs thyme
- 3-4 whole bay leaves

Instructions:

1. **Prepare the Fish:**
   - Rinse the fish under cold water and pat dry with paper towels. Score both sides of the fish with diagonal cuts (this helps the fish cook evenly and allows the flavors to penetrate).
2. **Season and Fry the Fish:**
   - Season the fish inside and out with salt and pepper.
   - Heat vegetable oil in a large skillet or frying pan over medium-high heat. Fry the fish on both sides until golden brown and cooked through, about 4-5 minutes per side depending on the thickness of the fish. Remove the fish from the pan and place on a plate lined with paper towels to drain excess oil.
3. **Prepare the Escovitch Sauce:**
   - In a medium saucepan, combine the vinegar, water, sugar, salt, allspice berries, black pepper, thyme sprigs, and bay leaves. Bring to a boil over medium-high heat, then reduce the heat and simmer for 3-4 minutes.
4. **Pickling the Vegetables:**
   - Add the sliced onion, bell pepper, carrot, and Scotch bonnet peppers to the simmering vinegar mixture.
   - Cook for another 2-3 minutes, stirring occasionally, until the vegetables are just tender but still crisp. Remove from heat.
5. **Assemble the Dish:**

- Arrange the fried fish on a serving platter.
- Spoon the escovitch sauce and pickled vegetables over the fish, covering it evenly.
6. **Serve:**
    - Fish Escovitch is traditionally served warm or at room temperature. Enjoy it as a main dish with rice and peas, boiled yams, or fried plantains. The tangy and spicy flavors of the escovitch sauce complement the delicate taste of the fried fish beautifully.

Fish Escovitch is a vibrant and flavorful dish that showcases the bold and distinctive tastes of Jamaican cuisine. It's perfect for sharing with family and friends, especially during gatherings or celebrations!

Pelau (One Pot Rice and Chicken)

Ingredients:

- 2 lbs chicken thighs and drumsticks, skin-on and bone-in
- 2 cups rice (long-grain or medium-grain)
- 1 cup pigeon peas (or substitute with kidney beans or black-eyed peas)
- 2 tablespoons vegetable oil
- 1 onion, chopped
- 4 cloves garlic, minced
- 1 bell pepper, chopped (red, green, or yellow)
- 1 medium carrot, diced
- 1 cup diced pumpkin or squash (optional)
- 2 tablespoons brown sugar
- 2 tablespoons soy sauce
- 2 tablespoons Worcestershire sauce
- 2 tablespoons tomato paste
- 2 cups coconut milk
- 2 cups chicken broth or water
- 2 sprigs thyme
- 2 whole cloves
- Salt and pepper, to taste
- Scotch bonnet pepper or hot pepper sauce (optional, for heat)
- Chopped fresh parsley or cilantro, for garnish

Instructions:

1. **Prepare the Chicken:**
   - Season the chicken pieces with salt and pepper. In a large pot or Dutch oven, heat vegetable oil over medium-high heat. Brown the chicken pieces on all sides until golden brown. Remove and set aside.
2. **Sauté Aromatics:**
   - In the same pot, add chopped onion, minced garlic, and bell pepper. Sauté for 3-4 minutes until softened and fragrant.
3. **Add Vegetables and Seasonings:**
   - Stir in diced carrot and pumpkin (if using). Cook for another 3-4 minutes.
   - Add brown sugar, soy sauce, Worcestershire sauce, and tomato paste. Mix well to combine.
4. **Add Rice and Liquid:**
   - Return the chicken pieces to the pot. Add rice and pigeon peas (or beans).
   - Pour in coconut milk and chicken broth (or water). Stir gently to combine all ingredients.
   - Add thyme sprigs and whole cloves. Season with salt and pepper to taste. If you like it spicy, add Scotch bonnet pepper or hot pepper sauce to your preference.
5. **Simmer the Pelau:**

- Bring the mixture to a boil, then reduce the heat to low. Cover the pot and let it simmer gently for 25-30 minutes, or until the rice is cooked and liquid is absorbed. Stir occasionally to prevent sticking.

6. **Finish and Serve:**
   - Once the rice is tender and fluffy, remove the pot from heat. Discard thyme sprigs and cloves.
   - Garnish with chopped fresh parsley or cilantro before serving.

Pelau is typically served hot as a main dish. It's a comforting and satisfying meal that captures the flavors of the Caribbean, perfect for sharing with family and friends. Enjoy your homemade Pelau with a side of coleslaw, fried plantains, or a fresh salad!

Guava BBQ Ribs

Ingredients:

- 2 racks of pork baby back ribs (about 4-5 lbs total)
- Salt and pepper, to taste

For the Guava BBQ Sauce:

- 1 cup guava jelly or guava paste
- 1/2 cup ketchup
- 1/4 cup brown sugar
- 1/4 cup apple cider vinegar
- 2 tablespoons soy sauce
- 1 tablespoon Worcestershire sauce
- 1 tablespoon Dijon mustard
- 2 cloves garlic, minced
- 1 teaspoon smoked paprika
- 1/2 teaspoon ground cumin
- 1/2 teaspoon ground ginger
- 1/4 teaspoon cayenne pepper (optional, for heat)
- Salt and pepper, to taste

Instructions:

1. **Prepare the Ribs:**
   - Remove the membrane from the back of the ribs, if not already done. Season the ribs generously with salt and pepper on both sides.
2. **Preheat the Oven:**
   - Preheat your oven to 300°F (150°C).
3. **Make the Guava BBQ Sauce:**
   - In a saucepan over medium heat, combine guava jelly (or paste), ketchup, brown sugar, apple cider vinegar, soy sauce, Worcestershire sauce, Dijon mustard, minced garlic, smoked paprika, ground cumin, ground ginger, and cayenne pepper (if using).
   - Stir well to combine and bring to a simmer. Cook for 8-10 minutes, stirring occasionally, until the sauce thickens slightly. Season with salt and pepper to taste. Remove from heat and set aside.
4. **Prepare the Ribs for Baking:**
   - Place the ribs on a large baking sheet lined with aluminum foil or parchment paper. Brush or spoon some of the guava BBQ sauce over the ribs, coating them evenly on both sides.
5. **Bake the Ribs:**

    - Cover the ribs tightly with aluminum foil and bake in the preheated oven for 2.5 to 3 hours, or until the meat is tender and cooked through. About halfway through cooking, remove the foil and baste the ribs with more guava BBQ sauce.
6. **Finish on the Grill (Optional):**
    - Preheat your grill to medium-high heat. Remove the ribs from the oven and carefully transfer them to the grill.
    - Grill the ribs for 3-4 minutes per side, brushing with more guava BBQ sauce and turning occasionally, until the sauce caramelizes and the ribs have a nice charred exterior. Watch carefully to avoid burning.
7. **Serve:**
    - Remove the ribs from the grill and let them rest for a few minutes before slicing into individual ribs or serving as whole racks.
    - Serve the Guava BBQ Ribs hot, with extra guava BBQ sauce on the side for dipping or drizzling.

Enjoy these Guava BBQ Ribs as a flavorful and tropical twist on classic barbecue ribs. They're perfect for a backyard cookout or special occasion, bringing the taste of the Caribbean to your table!

Coconut Shrimp

Ingredients:

- 1 lb large shrimp, peeled and deveined (tails left on or removed, depending on preference)
- 1 cup sweetened shredded coconut
- 1 cup panko breadcrumbs (or regular breadcrumbs)
- 1/2 cup all-purpose flour
- 1/2 teaspoon salt
- 1/4 teaspoon black pepper
- 2 large eggs
- Vegetable oil, for frying

Instructions:

1. **Prepare the Shrimp:**
   - Pat the shrimp dry with paper towels to remove excess moisture.
2. **Set Up Coating Stations:**
   - In three separate shallow bowls, prepare the coating stations:
     - Bowl 1: All-purpose flour, salt, and black pepper (mix together).
     - Bowl 2: Eggs, beaten.
     - Bowl 3: Sweetened shredded coconut and panko breadcrumbs (mix together).
3. **Coat the Shrimp:**
   - Dip each shrimp first into the flour mixture (bowl 1), shaking off any excess.
   - Next, dip the shrimp into the beaten eggs (bowl 2), allowing any excess to drip off.
   - Finally, coat the shrimp thoroughly in the coconut and breadcrumb mixture (bowl 3), pressing gently to adhere the coating.
4. **Fry the Coconut Shrimp:**
   - In a large skillet or frying pan, heat vegetable oil over medium-high heat until it reaches about 350°F (175°C).
   - Carefully place the coated shrimp into the hot oil, a few at a time, making sure not to overcrowd the pan.
   - Fry the shrimp for 2-3 minutes per side, or until the coating is golden brown and the shrimp is cooked through and pink. Use tongs to turn the shrimp halfway through cooking.
   - Remove the cooked shrimp from the oil and place them on a plate lined with paper towels to drain excess oil.
5. **Serve:**
   - Serve the coconut shrimp hot, as an appetizer or main dish.
   - Optionally, serve with a dipping sauce such as sweet chili sauce, mango salsa, or a creamy coconut lime sauce.
6. **Enjoy:**

- Enjoy the crispy and delicious coconut shrimp as a tropical treat that's perfect for any occasion!

Coconut shrimp is best served fresh and hot, maintaining its crispy exterior and tender shrimp inside. It's a crowd-pleasing dish that brings a taste of the tropics to your table!

Jamaican Brown Stew Chicken

Ingredients:

- 2 lbs chicken pieces (such as thighs and drumsticks), skin-on and bone-in
- Salt and pepper, to taste
- 2 tablespoons vegetable oil
- 1 onion, thinly sliced
- 3 cloves garlic, minced
- 1 bell pepper (red, green, or yellow), chopped
- 2 tomatoes, chopped
- 2 tablespoons brown sugar
- 2 tablespoons soy sauce
- 2 tablespoons Worcestershire sauce
- 1 tablespoon tomato paste
- 1 cup chicken broth or water
- 2 sprigs thyme
- 2-3 whole allspice berries
- 1 Scotch bonnet pepper (whole, optional, for flavor)

Instructions:

1. **Marinate the Chicken:**
   - Season the chicken pieces with salt and pepper. You can marinate them for at least 30 minutes to overnight in the refrigerator for more flavor.
2. **Brown the Chicken:**
   - Heat vegetable oil in a large Dutch oven or heavy-bottomed pot over medium-high heat. Brown the chicken pieces on all sides until golden brown. Work in batches if needed to avoid overcrowding the pot. Remove the chicken and set aside.
3. **Prepare the Sauce:**
   - In the same pot, add sliced onion, minced garlic, and chopped bell pepper. Sauté for 3-4 minutes until softened and fragrant.
4. **Add Seasonings and Liquid:**
   - Stir in chopped tomatoes, brown sugar, soy sauce, Worcestershire sauce, and tomato paste. Cook for another 2-3 minutes to combine flavors.
   - Pour in chicken broth (or water). Return the browned chicken pieces to the pot.
   - Add thyme sprigs, whole allspice berries, and Scotch bonnet pepper (if using). Stir gently to combine.
5. **Simmer the Stew:**
   - Bring the mixture to a boil, then reduce the heat to low. Cover the pot and let it simmer gently for 30-40 minutes, or until the chicken is tender and cooked through. Stir occasionally.
6. **Adjust Seasoning and Serve:**

- Taste the stew and adjust seasoning with salt and pepper if necessary. If you prefer a thicker sauce, you can simmer uncovered for a few more minutes.
- Remove the Scotch bonnet pepper, thyme sprigs, and allspice berries before serving.

7. **Serve:**
    - Jamaican Brown Stew Chicken is traditionally served hot, accompanied by rice and peas, steamed vegetables, or fried plantains.

Enjoy this Jamaican Brown Stew Chicken, rich in flavors and perfect for a comforting and satisfying meal that captures the essence of Caribbean cuisine!

Haitian Griot (Fried Pork)

Ingredients:

- 2 lbs pork shoulder, cut into 1-inch cubes
- 3 cloves garlic, minced
- 1 teaspoon salt
- 1 teaspoon black pepper
- 1 teaspoon dried thyme (or 2-3 sprigs fresh thyme, leaves only)
- 1 teaspoon dried oregano
- 1 teaspoon paprika
- 1/2 teaspoon cayenne pepper (adjust to taste)
- Juice of 1 lime (about 2 tablespoons)
- Juice of 1 orange (about 1/2 cup)
- 1/4 cup vinegar (white or apple cider vinegar)
- Vegetable oil, for frying

For serving:

- Pikliz (Haitian spicy pickled vegetables)
- Rice and beans (diri kole ak pwa) or rice and peas

Instructions:

1. **Marinate the Pork:**
   - In a large bowl, combine the pork cubes with minced garlic, salt, black pepper, dried thyme, dried oregano, paprika, cayenne pepper, lime juice, orange juice, and vinegar. Mix well to coat the pork evenly with the marinade.
   - Cover the bowl and refrigerate for at least 2 hours, or preferably overnight, to allow the flavors to develop.
2. **Fry the Griot:**
   - Heat vegetable oil in a large skillet or Dutch oven over medium-high heat. Add enough oil to generously cover the bottom of the pan.
   - Remove the marinated pork from the bowl, shaking off excess marinade. Reserve the marinade for later use.
   - Working in batches to avoid overcrowding the pan, fry the pork cubes in the hot oil until they are golden brown and crispy on all sides, about 6-8 minutes per batch.
   - Use a slotted spoon or tongs to transfer the fried pork (griot) to a plate lined with paper towels to drain excess oil.
3. **Make the Griot Sauce:**
   - After frying all the pork, pour the reserved marinade into the skillet. Bring to a boil, then reduce the heat and let it simmer for 5-7 minutes, stirring occasionally, until the sauce thickens slightly.
4. **Serve:**

- - Serve the Haitian Griot hot, accompanied by pikliz (spicy pickled vegetables) and rice and beans (diri kole ak pwa) or rice and peas.
  - Garnish with additional pikliz on the side for extra flavor and spice.

Haitian Griot is a flavorful and beloved dish that showcases the vibrant culinary traditions of Haiti. It's perfect for gatherings and celebrations, offering a delicious combination of crispy fried pork with tangy and spicy accents from the pikliz. Enjoy this authentic Haitian dish with family and friends!

Bahamian Conch Chowder

Ingredients:

- 1 lb conch meat, cleaned and diced (fresh or frozen, thawed)
- 2 tablespoons vegetable oil
- 1 onion, finely chopped
- 2-3 cloves garlic, minced
- 1 bell pepper (red, green, or yellow), chopped
- 2 celery stalks, chopped
- 1 carrot, diced
- 2 medium potatoes, peeled and diced
- 1 can (14 oz) diced tomatoes
- 4 cups fish or seafood broth (or chicken broth)
- 1 cup coconut milk
- 1 tablespoon tomato paste
- 1 bay leaf
- 1 teaspoon dried thyme (or 2-3 sprigs fresh thyme)
- 1/4 teaspoon cayenne pepper (adjust to taste)
- Salt and pepper, to taste
- Fresh parsley or cilantro, chopped, for garnish
- Lime wedges, for serving

Instructions:

1. **Prepare the Conch:**
    - If using fresh conch, tenderize it by pounding with a meat mallet or rolling pin until thin, then dice into small pieces. If using frozen conch, ensure it is fully thawed before using.
2. **Sauté Aromatics:**
    - In a large pot or Dutch oven, heat vegetable oil over medium heat. Add chopped onion, minced garlic, chopped bell pepper, celery, and carrot. Sauté for 5-7 minutes until the vegetables are softened.
3. **Add Potatoes and Tomatoes:**
    - Add diced potatoes and canned diced tomatoes (with their juices) to the pot. Stir well to combine with the sautéed vegetables.
4. **Simmer the Chowder:**
    - Pour in fish or seafood broth (or chicken broth), coconut milk, and tomato paste. Stir to combine. Add bay leaf, dried thyme (or fresh thyme), and cayenne pepper.
    - Bring the mixture to a boil, then reduce the heat to low. Cover the pot and let it simmer gently for 20-25 minutes, or until the potatoes are tender.
5. **Add Conch and Seasoning:**
    - Add the diced conch meat to the pot. Simmer for an additional 10-15 minutes, or until the conch is cooked through and tender.

- Taste the chowder and season with salt and pepper as needed. Adjust the cayenne pepper if you prefer more heat.
6. **Serve:**
    - Remove the bay leaf from the chowder before serving.
    - Ladle the Bahamian Conch Chowder into bowls. Garnish with chopped fresh parsley or cilantro.
    - Serve hot with lime wedges on the side for squeezing over the chowder.

Bahamian Conch Chowder is best enjoyed fresh and hot, with its rich flavors of seafood, coconut milk, and Caribbean spices. It's a comforting and satisfying soup that captures the essence of Bahamian cuisine. Enjoy this delightful dish on its own or with a side of crusty bread!

Curried Crab and Dumplings

Ingredients:

For the Curry Crab:

- 2 lbs crab (cleaned and cracked, or use crab meat)
- 2 tablespoons curry powder
- 1 onion, finely chopped
- 3 cloves garlic, minced
- 1 bell pepper (red, green, or yellow), chopped
- 1 tomato, chopped
- 2 tablespoons vegetable oil
- 1 cup coconut milk
- 1 cup seafood or chicken broth
- 1 tablespoon tomato paste
- 1 teaspoon ground turmeric
- 1 teaspoon ground cumin
- 1 teaspoon ground coriander
- 1/2 teaspoon cayenne pepper (adjust to taste)
- Salt and pepper, to taste
- Fresh cilantro or parsley, chopped (for garnish)
- Lime wedges, for serving

For the Dumplings:

- 1 cup all-purpose flour
- 1 teaspoon baking powder
- 1/2 teaspoon salt
- 1/2 cup water (approximately)

Instructions:

For the Curry Crab:

1. **Prepare the Curry Base:**
   - In a large pot or Dutch oven, heat vegetable oil over medium heat. Add chopped onion, minced garlic, and chopped bell pepper. Sauté for 3-4 minutes until softened.
2. **Add Spices:**
   - Stir in curry powder, ground turmeric, ground cumin, ground coriander, and cayenne pepper. Cook for another 1-2 minutes to toast the spices, stirring constantly to prevent burning.
3. **Make the Curry Sauce:**
   - Add chopped tomato and tomato paste to the pot. Cook for 2-3 minutes until the tomatoes start to break down.

4. **Cook the Crab:**
   - Add cleaned and cracked crab (or crab meat) to the pot. Stir to coat the crab with the curry mixture.
5. **Add Liquid:**
   - Pour in coconut milk and seafood or chicken broth. Stir well to combine. Bring the mixture to a simmer.
6. **Simmer the Curry:**
   - Reduce the heat to low. Cover the pot and let the curry simmer gently for 15-20 minutes, stirring occasionally, until the crab is cooked through and tender.
   - Taste the curry and adjust seasoning with salt and pepper as needed.

For the Dumplings:

1. **Prepare the Dough:**
   - In a mixing bowl, combine flour, baking powder, and salt. Gradually add water, stirring with a fork or your hands, until a soft dough forms. You may need slightly more or less water depending on humidity.
2. **Form the Dumplings:**
   - Divide the dough into small balls, about 1 inch in diameter. Roll each ball between your palms to smooth it out.
3. **Cook the Dumplings:**
   - Drop the dumplings into the simmering curry crab mixture. Cover the pot and let the dumplings cook for 10-12 minutes, or until they are cooked through and fluffy.
4. **Serve:**
   - Ladle the Curried Crab and Dumplings into bowls, ensuring each serving has a generous portion of crab, curry sauce, and dumplings.
   - Garnish with chopped fresh cilantro or parsley.
   - Serve hot with lime wedges on the side for squeezing over the dish.

Curried Crab and Dumplings is a comforting and flavorful dish that combines the richness of curry with the tender sweetness of crab meat and the hearty texture of dumplings. Enjoy this Caribbean delicacy with family and friends for a satisfying meal!

Trinidadian Callaloo

Ingredients:

- 1 lb dasheen leaves (taro leaves) or amaranth greens, washed and chopped
- 1 tablespoon vegetable oil
- 1 onion, finely chopped
- 3 cloves garlic, minced
- 1 bell pepper (any color), chopped
- 2 tomatoes, chopped
- 1 cup coconut milk
- 1 cup water or vegetable broth
- 1 scotch bonnet pepper, whole (optional, for heat)
- Salt and pepper, to taste
- Juice of 1 lime (optional, for serving)

Instructions:

1. **Prepare the Greens:**
   - Wash the dasheen leaves thoroughly and remove any tough stems. Chop the leaves into small pieces.
2. **Sauté Aromatics:**
   - In a large pot or Dutch oven, heat vegetable oil over medium heat. Add chopped onion, minced garlic, and chopped bell pepper. Sauté for 3-4 minutes until softened.
3. **Add Tomatoes:**
   - Add chopped tomatoes to the pot. Cook for another 2-3 minutes until the tomatoes begin to break down.
4. **Cook the Callaloo:**
   - Add the chopped dasheen leaves (or amaranth greens) to the pot. Stir well to combine with the sautéed aromatics.
5. **Add Coconut Milk and Liquid:**
   - Pour in coconut milk and water (or vegetable broth). Stir to combine. Add a whole scotch bonnet pepper (optional) for added flavor and heat.
6. **Simmer the Callaloo:**
   - Bring the mixture to a boil, then reduce the heat to low. Cover the pot and let it simmer gently for 20-25 minutes, stirring occasionally, until the greens are tender and cooked down.
7. **Season and Serve:**
   - Season the callaloo with salt and pepper to taste. If desired, squeeze fresh lime juice over the callaloo before serving for added brightness.
8. **Serve:**
   - Trinidadian Callaloo is traditionally served hot as a side dish or main meal, accompanied by rice and peas, fried plantains, or bread.

Enjoy this Trinidadian Callaloo, rich in flavors and nutrients, as a taste of Caribbean cuisine that's both comforting and satisfying!

Jamaican Steamed Fish

Ingredients:

- 2 lbs whole fish (such as snapper, tilapia, or grouper), cleaned and scaled
- 1 lime, juiced
- Salt and black pepper, to taste
- 2 tablespoons vegetable oil
- 1 onion, thinly sliced
- 2 cloves garlic, minced
- 1 bell pepper (red, green, or yellow), thinly sliced
- 1 medium tomato, sliced
- 1 scotch bonnet pepper, whole or sliced (adjust to taste)
- 1 sprig thyme
- 1/2 teaspoon ground allspice (pimento)
- 1/2 teaspoon ground ginger
- 1 cup fish or vegetable broth
- 1/2 cup coconut milk
- 1 tablespoon butter (optional)
- Fresh cilantro or parsley, chopped, for garnish
- Lime wedges, for serving

Instructions:

1. **Prepare the Fish:**
   - Rinse the whole fish under cold water and pat dry with paper towels. Score the fish on both sides with diagonal cuts. Rub the fish inside and out with lime juice, salt, and black pepper. Let it marinate for about 15-20 minutes.
2. **Sauté Aromatics:**
   - In a large, deep skillet or Dutch oven, heat vegetable oil over medium heat. Add sliced onion, minced garlic, and sliced bell pepper. Sauté for 3-4 minutes until softened.
3. **Assemble the Dish:**
   - Arrange the sliced tomato, whole scotch bonnet pepper (or sliced, if using), and thyme sprig in the skillet, creating a bed of vegetables and aromatics.
4. **Steam the Fish:**
   - Place the marinated fish on top of the bed of vegetables in the skillet. Sprinkle ground allspice and ground ginger over the fish.
   - Pour fish or vegetable broth and coconut milk around the fish. Cover the skillet with a lid.
5. **Cook the Fish:**
   - Bring the liquid to a simmer over medium-low heat. Steam the fish gently for 15-20 minutes, or until the fish is cooked through and flakes easily with a fork. Cooking time will vary depending on the size and thickness of the fish.
6. **Finish the Dish:**

- Optionally, dot the top of the fish with butter for added richness and flavor. Remove the skillet from heat.
7. **Serve:**
    - Carefully transfer the steamed fish and vegetables to serving plates. Garnish with chopped fresh cilantro or parsley.
    - Serve hot with lime wedges on the side for squeezing over the fish.

Jamaican Steamed Fish is often served with rice and peas or boiled dumplings, providing a complete and satisfying meal. Enjoy the delicate flavors and tender texture of the fish, complemented by the aromatic spices and vegetables in this traditional Caribbean dish!

Souse (Pickled Pork)

Ingredients:

- 2 lbs pork (shoulder or belly), cut into bite-sized pieces
- 1 cup lime or lemon juice (about 8-10 limes or lemons)
- 2 cups water
- 1 onion, thinly sliced
- 2-3 cloves garlic, minced
- 1-2 scotch bonnet peppers, whole or sliced (adjust to taste)
- 1 cucumber, thinly sliced (optional)
- 1 green bell pepper, thinly sliced
- 1/2 cup chopped fresh parsley or cilantro
- Salt and black pepper, to taste
- 1 tablespoon mustard seeds (optional)
- 1 teaspoon ground allspice (pimento)
- 1 teaspoon ground cloves
- 1 teaspoon ground black pepper

Instructions:

1. **Prepare the Pork:**
   - Rinse the pork pieces under cold water and place them in a large bowl. Cover with cold water and add half of the lime or lemon juice. Let it soak for 10-15 minutes.
2. **Boil the Pork:**
   - Transfer the pork and soaking liquid to a large pot. Add enough water to cover the pork by about an inch. Bring to a boil over medium-high heat, then reduce the heat to low and let it simmer for 1.5 to 2 hours, or until the pork is tender and cooked through.
3. **Prepare the Pickling Liquid:**
   - In a separate bowl, combine the remaining lime or lemon juice with 2 cups of water. Add minced garlic, sliced onion, sliced scotch bonnet peppers, cucumber slices (if using), green bell pepper slices, chopped parsley or cilantro, mustard seeds (if using), ground allspice, ground cloves, and ground black pepper. Mix well.
4. **Pickling Process:**
   - Once the pork is cooked and tender, drain it from the cooking liquid and transfer it to a large non-reactive bowl (glass or ceramic).
   - Pour the prepared pickling liquid mixture over the pork, ensuring it is completely submerged. Add salt and additional black pepper to taste if needed.
   - Cover the bowl with plastic wrap or a tight-fitting lid and refrigerate for at least 4 hours, preferably overnight, to allow the flavors to meld and the pork to absorb the pickling marinade.
5. **Serve:**

- Serve the Barbadian Souse chilled as a cold appetizer or snack. It is traditionally enjoyed with bread, crackers, or rice.

Barbadian Souse is known for its tangy, spicy, and aromatic flavors from the pickling liquid and spices. It's a refreshing dish that's perfect for warm weather or as part of a festive spread. Adjust the spiciness to your preference by adding more or fewer scotch bonnet peppers. Enjoy this traditional Caribbean dish!

Trinidadian Buss Up Shut (Paratha Roti)

Ingredients:

- 3 cups all-purpose flour
- 1 teaspoon baking powder
- 1/2 teaspoon salt
- 1 cup water (approximately)
- 1/4 cup vegetable oil (plus extra for cooking)
- 1/4 cup melted butter or ghee

Instructions:

1. **Prepare the Dough:**
   - In a large mixing bowl, combine the all-purpose flour, baking powder, and salt.
   - Gradually add water to the flour mixture, mixing with your hands or a spoon, until a soft dough forms. You may need slightly more or less water depending on humidity.
2. **Knead the Dough:**
   - Turn the dough out onto a lightly floured surface. Knead the dough for about 5-7 minutes until it is smooth and elastic. Cover the dough with a clean kitchen towel and let it rest for 30 minutes.
3. **Shape the Dough:**
   - Divide the rested dough into 8 equal portions. Roll each portion into a ball. Lightly coat each ball with vegetable oil to prevent sticking.
4. **Roll Out the Roti:**
   - Take one dough ball and roll it out on a lightly floured surface into a thin circle or oval shape, about 1/8 inch thick. Brush the surface with melted butter or ghee, then sprinkle lightly with flour.
5. **Fold and Coil the Roti:**
   - Starting from one edge, make a series of small pleats along the length of the dough, folding it accordion-style. Roll up the folded dough into a tight coil (similar to rolling up a rug).
6. **Rest and Repeat:**
   - Place the coiled dough ball on a plate and cover it with a clean kitchen towel. Repeat the process with the remaining dough portions.
7. **Roll Out and Cook the Roti:**
   - Take one coiled dough ball and gently flatten it with your palm. Roll it out again on a lightly floured surface into a thin circle, about 1/8 inch thick.
8. **Cook the Roti:**
   - Heat a non-stick skillet or tava over medium-high heat. Place the rolled-out roti on the hot skillet. Cook for about 1-2 minutes on each side, or until golden brown spots appear and the roti puffs up.
9. **Finish and Serve:**

- - Brush both sides of the cooked roti with melted butter or ghee as it comes off the skillet.
  - Stack the cooked roti on a plate and cover with a clean kitchen towel to keep them warm and soft.
  - Serve Trinidadian Buss Up Shut (Paratha Roti) hot with your favorite curry, stew, or side dish.

Trinidadian Buss Up Shut is traditionally torn into pieces ("bussed up") and used to scoop up curries and other dishes. Its flaky layers and buttery texture make it a delightful accompaniment to any Trinidadian meal. Enjoy!

Curry Shrimp

Ingredients:

- 1 lb shrimp, peeled and deveined
- 2 tablespoons curry powder
- 1 onion, finely chopped
- 3 cloves garlic, minced
- 1 bell pepper (any color), chopped
- 1 tomato, chopped
- 1 cup coconut milk
- 1/2 cup water or seafood broth
- 2 tablespoons vegetable oil
- 1 scotch bonnet pepper, whole (optional, for heat)
- 1 teaspoon ground turmeric
- 1 teaspoon ground cumin
- 1 teaspoon ground coriander
- 1/2 teaspoon paprika
- Salt and pepper, to taste
- Fresh cilantro or parsley, chopped, for garnish
- Lime wedges, for serving

Instructions:

1. **Prepare the Shrimp:**
    - Rinse the shrimp under cold water and pat dry with paper towels. Season with salt and pepper.
2. **Sauté Aromatics:**
    - In a large skillet or Dutch oven, heat vegetable oil over medium heat. Add chopped onion and bell pepper. Sauté for 3-4 minutes until softened.
3. **Add Spices:**
    - Stir in curry powder, ground turmeric, ground cumin, ground coriander, and paprika. Cook for 1-2 minutes until fragrant, stirring constantly.
4. **Cook the Curry:**
    - Add minced garlic and chopped tomato to the skillet. Cook for another 2-3 minutes until the tomatoes begin to break down.
5. **Simmer the Shrimp:**
    - Pour in coconut milk and water (or seafood broth). Stir well to combine. Add a whole scotch bonnet pepper (optional) for added flavor and heat.
    - Bring the mixture to a simmer, then reduce the heat to low. Let it simmer gently for 5-7 minutes to allow the flavors to meld.
6. **Add Shrimp:**
    - Add the seasoned shrimp to the skillet. Stir gently to coat the shrimp with the curry sauce.
7. **Cook Shrimp:**

- Cook the shrimp for 5-7 minutes, or until they turn pink and opaque. Be careful not to overcook them, as shrimp can become rubbery if cooked too long.
8. **Adjust Seasoning:**
    - Taste the curry shrimp and adjust seasoning with salt and pepper as needed.
9. **Serve:**
    - Remove the scotch bonnet pepper (if used) before serving.
    - Garnish with chopped fresh cilantro or parsley.
    - Serve hot with lime wedges on the side for squeezing over the curry shrimp.

Curry Shrimp pairs wonderfully with rice, roti, or bread to soak up the flavorful sauce. It's a comforting and aromatic dish that brings the taste of the Caribbean right to your table. Enjoy this delicious Curry Shrimp with family and friends!

Rasta Pasta

Ingredients:

- 8 oz penne pasta (or any pasta of your choice)
- 1 lb chicken breasts, cut into strips (optional; can be omitted for a vegetarian version)
- 2 tablespoons jerk seasoning (for seasoning the chicken, optional)
- 2 tablespoons vegetable oil
- 1 onion, finely chopped
- 3 cloves garlic, minced
- 1 bell pepper (red, green, or yellow), thinly sliced
- 1 cup coconut milk
- 1 cup heavy cream (or substitute with coconut cream for a dairy-free option)
- 1 tablespoon jerk seasoning (adjust to taste)
- 1/2 teaspoon ground turmeric
- 1/2 teaspoon paprika
- Salt and pepper, to taste
- Fresh parsley or cilantro, chopped, for garnish

Instructions:

1. **Cook the Pasta:**
   - Cook the pasta according to package instructions in a large pot of salted boiling water until al dente. Drain and set aside.
2. **Prepare the Chicken (Optional):**
   - Season the chicken strips with jerk seasoning (or your preferred seasoning blend). Heat 1 tablespoon of vegetable oil in a large skillet over medium-high heat. Cook the chicken until browned and cooked through, about 5-7 minutes per side. Remove from the skillet and set aside.
3. **Make the Sauce:**
   - In the same skillet, heat the remaining 1 tablespoon of vegetable oil over medium heat. Add chopped onion and sliced bell pepper. Sauté for 3-4 minutes until softened.
4. **Add Aromatics:**
   - Add minced garlic, ground turmeric, and paprika to the skillet. Cook for another 1-2 minutes until fragrant, stirring constantly.
5. **Add Coconut Milk and Cream:**
   - Pour in coconut milk and heavy cream (or coconut cream). Stir well to combine. Bring the mixture to a simmer, then reduce the heat to low.
6. **Season the Sauce:**
   - Stir in jerk seasoning, salt, and pepper to taste. Adjust the seasoning according to your preference for spiciness.
7. **Combine Pasta and Sauce:**
   - Add the cooked pasta (and cooked chicken, if using) to the skillet with the sauce. Toss everything together gently until the pasta is well coated with the sauce.

8. **Serve:**
    - Remove from heat and garnish with chopped fresh parsley or cilantro.
    - Serve hot, optionally with additional jerk seasoning on the side for those who prefer extra spice.

Rasta Pasta is a vibrant and creamy dish that brings together the bold flavors of Caribbean spices with pasta, creating a unique and satisfying meal. Enjoy this flavorful Rasta Pasta with your favorite side salad or garlic bread for a complete dining experience!

Goat Water (Stewed Goat Soup)

Ingredients:

- 2 lbs goat meat, cut into bite-sized pieces (bone-in for more flavor)
- 2 tablespoons vegetable oil
- 1 onion, finely chopped
- 4 cloves garlic, minced
- 2 tomatoes, chopped
- 1 bell pepper (any color), chopped
- 2 celery stalks, chopped
- 2 carrots, diced
- 2 potatoes, peeled and diced
- 1 scotch bonnet pepper, whole (optional, for heat)
- 1 tablespoon tomato paste
- 1 tablespoon Worcestershire sauce
- 1 teaspoon dried thyme (or 2-3 sprigs fresh thyme)
- 1 teaspoon ground allspice (pimento)
- 1/2 teaspoon ground cloves
- 1/2 teaspoon ground nutmeg
- Salt and pepper, to taste
- 6 cups water or beef broth
- Juice of 1 lime or lemon
- Fresh parsley or cilantro, chopped, for garnish
- Cooked rice or dumplings, for serving (optional)

Instructions:

1. **Prepare the Goat Meat:**
   - Rinse the goat meat under cold water and pat dry with paper towels. Season with salt and pepper.
2. **Sear the Goat Meat:**
   - In a large Dutch oven or heavy-bottomed pot, heat vegetable oil over medium-high heat. Add the seasoned goat meat in batches and sear until browned on all sides. Remove and set aside.
3. **Sauté Aromatics:**
   - In the same pot, add chopped onion, minced garlic, chopped tomatoes, and chopped bell pepper. Sauté for 3-4 minutes until softened.
4. **Add Spices and Tomato Paste:**
   - Stir in tomato paste, Worcestershire sauce, dried thyme, ground allspice, ground cloves, and ground nutmeg. Cook for another 1-2 minutes until fragrant, stirring constantly.
5. **Simmer the Goat Water:**

- Return the seared goat meat to the pot. Pour in water or beef broth, ensuring the meat is fully submerged. Add the whole scotch bonnet pepper (if using) for added heat. Bring the mixture to a boil.

6. **Reduce Heat and Simmer:**
   - Reduce the heat to low, cover the pot, and let it simmer gently for 2-2.5 hours, or until the goat meat is tender and almost falling off the bone. Stir occasionally and skim off any foam that rises to the surface.

7. **Add Vegetables:**
   - Add chopped celery, diced carrots, and diced potatoes to the pot. Continue to simmer, uncovered, for another 30-45 minutes, or until the vegetables are tender and the stew has thickened slightly.

8. **Finish and Serve:**
   - Remove the scotch bonnet pepper (if used) from the pot. Stir in the juice of 1 lime or lemon.
   - Taste and adjust seasoning with salt and pepper as needed.
   - Serve hot, garnished with chopped fresh parsley or cilantro.
   - Optionally, serve Goat Water with cooked rice or dumplings on the side for a hearty meal.

Goat Water is a delicious and warming dish that brings together the rich flavors of tender goat meat with aromatic spices and hearty vegetables. It's perfect for a comforting meal on a cool day, showcasing the diverse and flavorful cuisine of the Caribbean. Enjoy!

Caribbean Fish Cakes

Ingredients:

- 1 lb salted cod (saltfish)
- 2 cups mashed potatoes (about 2 medium potatoes)
- 1 onion, finely chopped
- 2 cloves garlic, minced
- 1 scotch bonnet pepper, finely chopped (adjust to taste)
- 1/4 cup fresh parsley, chopped
- 1/4 cup fresh cilantro, chopped
- 1 teaspoon ground allspice (pimento)
- 1/2 teaspoon ground black pepper
- 1/2 teaspoon baking powder
- 1 egg, beaten
- Vegetable oil, for frying

Instructions:

1. **Prepare the Salted Cod:**
    - Rinse the salted cod under cold water to remove excess salt. Place it in a large bowl and cover with cold water. Let it soak for at least 4 hours, changing the water 2-3 times to remove more salt. Alternatively, soak overnight in the refrigerator.
2. **Boil and Flake the Cod:**
    - Drain the soaked salted cod and place it in a pot of fresh water. Bring to a boil, then reduce the heat and simmer for about 15-20 minutes, or until the cod flakes easily with a fork.
    - Drain the cod and let it cool slightly. Remove any bones and skin, then flake the cod into small pieces using a fork.
3. **Prepare the Fish Cake Mixture:**
    - In a large mixing bowl, combine the flaked cod with mashed potatoes, chopped onion, minced garlic, chopped scotch bonnet pepper, chopped parsley, chopped cilantro, ground allspice, ground black pepper, and baking powder. Mix well until all ingredients are evenly incorporated.
4. **Form the Fish Cakes:**
    - Take a small handful of the fish cake mixture and shape it into a round patty, about 2-3 inches in diameter. Repeat with the remaining mixture to make 10-12 fish cakes.
5. **Cook the Fish Cakes:**
    - Heat vegetable oil in a large skillet over medium heat. Add the fish cakes in batches, cooking for 3-4 minutes on each side, or until golden brown and crispy.
    - Remove the fish cakes from the skillet and place them on a plate lined with paper towels to drain excess oil.
6. **Serve:**

- Serve Caribbean Fish Cakes hot, garnished with additional chopped parsley or cilantro if desired.
- They are typically enjoyed on their own or with a dipping sauce like tartar sauce, mango chutney, or a spicy aioli.

Caribbean Fish Cakes are flavorful and aromatic, with a crispy exterior and a tender, savory interior. They make a perfect appetizer for parties or gatherings, showcasing the delicious flavors of Caribbean cuisine. Enjoy these tasty fish cakes with friends and family!

Barbadian Macaroni Pie

Ingredients:

- 8 oz elbow macaroni (or pasta of your choice)
- 2 cups grated cheddar cheese (preferably sharp)
- 2 cups milk
- 2 eggs, beaten
- 1/4 cup butter, melted
- 1/4 cup all-purpose flour
- 1 onion, finely chopped
- 2 cloves garlic, minced
- 1/4 teaspoon grated nutmeg
- Salt and pepper, to taste
- 1/4 cup breadcrumbs (optional, for topping)

Instructions:

1. **Preheat the Oven:**
    - Preheat your oven to 350°F (175°C). Grease a 9x13 inch baking dish or similar oven-proof dish.
2. **Cook the Macaroni:**
    - Cook the elbow macaroni in a large pot of salted boiling water according to package instructions until al dente. Drain and set aside.
3. **Prepare the Cheese Sauce:**
    - In a medium saucepan, melt the butter over medium heat. Add the chopped onion and minced garlic. Sauté for 3-4 minutes until softened.
    - Stir in the all-purpose flour and cook for 1-2 minutes, stirring constantly, to make a roux.
    - Gradually whisk in the milk, a little at a time, until smooth and thickened. Cook for 5-7 minutes, stirring occasionally, until the sauce coats the back of a spoon.
    - Remove from heat and stir in the grated cheddar cheese until melted and smooth. Season with grated nutmeg, salt, and pepper to taste.
4. **Combine and Bake:**
    - In a large mixing bowl, combine the cooked macaroni with the cheese sauce, stirring gently until evenly coated.
    - Add the beaten eggs to the macaroni mixture and stir until well combined.
5. **Bake the Macaroni Pie:**
    - Transfer the macaroni mixture to the prepared baking dish, spreading it out evenly.
    - If desired, sprinkle breadcrumbs evenly over the top for a crispy topping.
    - Bake in the preheated oven for 30-35 minutes, or until the top is golden brown and the edges are bubbling.
6. **Serve:**

- Remove from the oven and let the Barbadian Macaroni Pie cool slightly before serving.
- Serve warm as a side dish or main course, alongside salads or other Caribbean-inspired dishes.

Barbadian Macaroni Pie is creamy, cheesy, and satisfying, making it a favorite comfort food that pairs well with various meats and vegetables. Enjoy the rich flavors and comforting textures of this Barbadian classic!

Pelau (One Pot Rice and Beef)

Ingredients:

- 2 cups long-grain rice
- 1 lb beef (or chicken), cut into cubes
- 1 cup pigeon peas (or substitute with kidney beans)
- 1 onion, finely chopped
- 3 cloves garlic, minced
- 1 bell pepper, chopped
- 2 medium carrots, diced
- 3 tbsp vegetable oil
- 2 tbsp brown sugar
- 2 tbsp soy sauce
- 2 cups coconut milk
- 2 cups beef or chicken broth (or water)
- 1 tbsp fresh thyme leaves
- 1 scotch bonnet pepper (optional, for heat)
- Salt and pepper to taste

Instructions:

1. **Marinate the meat:** Season the beef cubes with salt, pepper, and a bit of soy sauce. Let it marinate for at least 30 minutes (preferably longer, if time allows).
2. **Prepare the peas:** If using dried pigeon peas, soak them overnight. Alternatively, use canned pigeon peas or kidney beans, drained and rinsed.
3. **Cooking the Pelau:**
    - Heat the vegetable oil in a large heavy-bottomed pot over medium-high heat.
    - Add the brown sugar to the hot oil and let it caramelize to a deep golden brown (this gives the Pelau its distinctive color and flavor).
    - Carefully add the seasoned meat to the pot and brown it on all sides.
    - Once the meat is browned, add the chopped onion, garlic, bell pepper, and carrots. Sauté for a few minutes until the vegetables start to soften.
4. **Add the rice and peas:**
    - Stir in the rice and pigeon peas (or kidney beans) until they are well coated with the oil and flavors from the pot.
    - Pour in the coconut milk and broth (or water). Stir well to combine.
5. **Season and simmer:**
    - Season with salt and pepper to taste.
    - Add the fresh thyme leaves and scotch bonnet pepper (whole, if you want flavor without too much heat; chopped if you like it spicy).
    - Bring the mixture to a boil, then reduce the heat to low, cover the pot, and let it simmer for about 20-25 minutes, or until the rice is cooked and most of the liquid is absorbed. Stir occasionally to prevent sticking.

6. **Serve:**
    - Once the rice is cooked and the liquid is absorbed, remove the pot from the heat.
    - Let the Pelau rest for a few minutes before serving. Fluff the rice with a fork and serve hot.

Tips:

- Pelau is often served with a side of coleslaw or a fresh salad.
- Adjust the amount of scotch bonnet pepper according to your spice preference.
- You can customize this recipe by adding other vegetables like green beans or spinach.

Enjoy your homemade Pelau, a delightful blend of flavors that captures the essence of Caribbean cuisine!

Curried Lobster

Ingredients:

- 2 lobsters (about 1 to 1.5 lbs each), cleaned and cut into pieces
- 2 tbsp curry powder (adjust to taste)
- 1 onion, finely chopped
- 3 cloves garlic, minced
- 1-inch piece of ginger, minced
- 1 tomato, chopped
- 1 can (14 oz) coconut milk
- 1 cup seafood or chicken broth
- 1 tbsp vegetable oil
- 1 tbsp tomato paste
- 1 scotch bonnet pepper, whole (optional, for heat)
- Fresh cilantro or parsley, chopped (for garnish)
- Salt and pepper to taste

Instructions:

1. **Prepare the lobster:**
    - Clean the lobsters thoroughly. Remove the claws and tail, and cut the body into pieces. Keep the shells intact for presentation, if desired.
2. **Marinate the lobster:**
    - In a bowl, toss the lobster pieces with 1 tablespoon of curry powder and a pinch of salt. Set aside while you prepare the other ingredients.
3. **Cooking the curry:**
    - Heat the vegetable oil in a large pan or pot over medium heat.
    - Add the chopped onion and sauté until translucent, about 3-4 minutes.
    - Stir in the minced garlic and ginger, and cook for another 1-2 minutes until fragrant.
    - Add the remaining curry powder and tomato paste. Stir well to combine and cook for another minute to toast the spices.
4. **Add the lobster:**
    - Add the marinated lobster pieces to the pan. Sauté for 2-3 minutes, stirring frequently, until the lobster begins to turn opaque.
5. **Simmering:**
    - Pour in the coconut milk and seafood or chicken broth. Stir to combine.
    - Add the chopped tomato and whole scotch bonnet pepper (if using).
    - Season with salt and pepper to taste.
    - Bring the mixture to a simmer, then reduce the heat to low. Cover the pan and let it simmer gently for about 8-10 minutes, or until the lobster is fully cooked and tender.
6. **Finish and serve:**

- Once the lobster is cooked through, remove the pan from heat.
- Discard the scotch bonnet pepper (if used).
- Garnish with chopped fresh cilantro or parsley.
- Serve hot, either on its own or with steamed rice or crusty bread to soak up the flavorful sauce.

Tips:

- Adjust the amount of curry powder and scotch bonnet pepper according to your spice preference.
- You can customize the vegetables by adding bell peppers, spinach, or peas to the curry.
- Be careful not to overcook the lobster to maintain its tender texture.

Enjoy your homemade curried lobster, a delightful dish that showcases the luxurious flavor of lobster with the exotic spices of curry!

Saltfish Buljol

Ingredients:

- 1 lb salted cod (saltfish)
- 1 large onion, finely chopped
- 1 tomato, finely chopped
- 1 bell pepper (any color), finely chopped
- 1-2 scallions (green onions), finely chopped
- 1-2 cloves garlic, minced
- 1/4 cup fresh cilantro or parsley, chopped
- 1/4 cup olive oil (or vegetable oil)
- Juice of 1 lime or lemon
- 1/4 tsp black pepper
- Hot pepper sauce or chopped scotch bonnet pepper (optional, for heat)
- Crusty bread or fried bake, for serving

Instructions:

1. **Prepare the saltfish:**
   - Rinse the saltfish under cold water to remove excess salt. Place it in a bowl and cover with cold water. Let it soak for 1-2 hours, changing the water 2-3 times. This process helps to rehydrate and desalinate the fish.
2. **Cook the saltfish:**
   - After soaking, drain the saltfish and place it in a pot of fresh water. Bring the water to a boil, then reduce the heat and simmer for about 15-20 minutes, or until the fish flakes easily with a fork.
   - Drain the fish and let it cool slightly. Remove any bones and skin, then shred the fish into small pieces with your fingers or a fork.
3. **Prepare the vegetables:**
   - In a large bowl, combine the chopped onion, tomato, bell pepper, scallions, minced garlic, and chopped cilantro or parsley.
4. **Combine and season:**
   - Add the shredded saltfish to the bowl of vegetables.
   - Drizzle the olive oil over the mixture.
   - Squeeze the lime or lemon juice over the mixture.
   - Season with black pepper.
   - If desired, add a few dashes of hot pepper sauce or chopped scotch bonnet pepper for extra heat.
5. **Mix thoroughly:**
   - Gently toss all the ingredients together until well combined. Taste and adjust seasoning if needed.
6. **Serve:**

- Serve the Saltfish Buljol at room temperature or chilled, alongside slices of crusty bread or fried bake.

Tips:

- Saltfish can vary in saltiness, so adjust the soaking time and number of water changes accordingly.
- You can customize this dish by adding other vegetables like cucumber, celery, or avocado.
- Saltfish Buljol is often enjoyed as a breakfast dish or as a side with fried plantains or avocado slices.

Enjoy your Saltfish Buljol, a delicious and refreshing dish that celebrates the flavors of the Caribbean!

Caribbean Stewed Peas

Ingredients:

- 2 cups dried red kidney beans (or 2 cans, drained and rinsed)
- 1 onion, finely chopped
- 3 cloves garlic, minced
- 1 bell pepper (any color), chopped
- 2 tomatoes, chopped
- 1 sprig thyme (or 1 tsp dried thyme)
- 2-3 tbsp vegetable oil
- 1/2 cup coconut milk
- 2 cups vegetable or chicken broth (or water)
- 1 tbsp tomato paste
- 1/2 tsp ground allspice
- 1/2 tsp smoked paprika (optional)
- Salt and pepper, to taste
- Scotch bonnet pepper or hot sauce (optional, for heat)
- Fresh cilantro or parsley, chopped (for garnish)

Instructions:

1. **Prepare the beans:**
   - If using dried beans, soak them overnight in water. Drain and rinse the beans before cooking.
   - If using canned beans, drain and rinse them thoroughly.
2. **Cooking the stew:**
   - In a large pot or Dutch oven, heat the vegetable oil over medium heat.
   - Add the chopped onion and bell pepper. Sauté for 3-4 minutes until softened.
   - Add the minced garlic and sauté for another minute until fragrant.
3. **Add the tomatoes and seasonings:**
   - Stir in the chopped tomatoes, thyme, ground allspice, and smoked paprika (if using).
   - Cook for 2-3 minutes until the tomatoes start to break down.
4. **Incorporate the beans:**
   - Add the drained and rinsed kidney beans to the pot. Stir to combine with the vegetables and spices.
5. **Simmering:**
   - Pour in the coconut milk and vegetable or chicken broth (or water).
   - Stir in the tomato paste.
   - Season with salt and pepper to taste.
   - If you like your stew spicy, add a whole scotch bonnet pepper (pierced) or a few dashes of hot sauce.
6. **Cook until tender:**

- Bring the mixture to a boil, then reduce the heat to low. Cover the pot and let it simmer gently for 1 to 1.5 hours, or until the beans are tender and the stew has thickened to your desired consistency. Stir occasionally and add more liquid if needed.
7. **Finish and serve:**
    - Once the beans are tender and the stew has thickened, taste and adjust seasoning if necessary.
    - Remove the scotch bonnet pepper (if used) before serving.
    - Garnish with chopped fresh cilantro or parsley.

Tips:

- Serve Caribbean Stewed Peas hot, alongside rice, fried plantains, or bread.
- For a meatier version, you can add diced smoked ham, salt pork, or cooked sausage during the cooking process.
- This dish can be made ahead of time and tastes even better the next day as the flavors continue to meld.

Enjoy your Caribbean Stewed Peas, a comforting and satisfying dish rich in Caribbean flavors!

Ackee Salad

Ingredients:

- 1 can (approx. 20 oz) ackee, drained and rinsed (fresh ackee can also be used if available)
- 1 bell pepper (any color), diced
- 1 small red onion, finely chopped
- 1 medium tomato, diced
- 1/2 cucumber, diced
- 1/4 cup fresh cilantro or parsley, chopped
- Juice of 1 lime or lemon
- 2 tbsp extra virgin olive oil
- Salt and pepper, to taste
- Hot pepper sauce (optional, for heat)

Instructions:

1. **Prepare the ackee:**
   - If using canned ackee, drain and rinse it thoroughly under cold water to remove any excess brine. If using fresh ackee, boil it for 15 minutes, discard the water, and rinse the ackee before use.
2. **Combine ingredients:**
   - In a large mixing bowl, gently combine the drained ackee with diced bell pepper, red onion, tomato, cucumber, and chopped cilantro or parsley.
3. **Dress the salad:**
   - In a small bowl, whisk together the lime or lemon juice, extra virgin olive oil, salt, and pepper to make the dressing.
   - Pour the dressing over the ackee and vegetable mixture. Toss gently to coat all ingredients evenly.
4. **Adjust seasoning:**
   - Taste the salad and adjust seasoning if needed. Add a few dashes of hot pepper sauce if you prefer a spicier salad.
5. **Chill and serve:**
   - Cover the ackee salad and refrigerate for at least 30 minutes to allow the flavors to meld.
   - Serve chilled as a refreshing side dish or as a light meal on its own.

Tips:

- Ackee has a delicate texture, so gently toss the salad to avoid breaking up the ackee too much.
- Customize the salad by adding diced avocado, mango, or pineapple for extra sweetness and texture.

- This salad pairs well with grilled fish, jerk chicken, or served alongside rice and peas for a complete Caribbean meal.

Enjoy your Ackee Salad, a vibrant and flavorful dish that highlights the unique taste of ackee with fresh vegetables and herbs!

Barbadian Flying Fish Cutter

Ingredients:

- 4 fresh flying fish fillets (substitute with another white fish if flying fish isn't available)
- 4 sandwich rolls or Bajan salt bread rolls (or any crusty rolls)
- 1 cup all-purpose flour
- 1 tsp Bajan seasoning (or use a blend of garlic powder, onion powder, paprika, thyme, and black pepper)
- Salt and pepper, to taste
- Vegetable oil, for frying
- Lettuce leaves
- Sliced tomatoes
- Sliced onions
- Hot pepper sauce or Bajan pepper sauce (optional, for serving)

Instructions:

1. **Prepare the flying fish:**
    - Rinse the flying fish fillets and pat them dry with paper towels.
    - In a shallow bowl, mix together the flour, Bajan seasoning, salt, and pepper.
    - Dredge each fish fillet in the seasoned flour mixture, shaking off any excess.
2. **Fry the fish:**
    - Heat vegetable oil in a frying pan over medium-high heat.
    - Carefully place the fish fillets in the hot oil and fry for about 3-4 minutes on each side, or until golden brown and cooked through.
    - Remove the fish from the oil and place them on paper towels to drain excess oil.
3. **Assemble the cutter:**
    - Slice the sandwich rolls horizontally.
    - Layer each roll with lettuce leaves, sliced tomatoes, and sliced onions.
    - Place a fried fish fillet on each roll.
4. **Serve:**
    - Optionally, add a few drops of hot pepper sauce or Bajan pepper sauce on top of the fish.
    - Serve the Flying Fish Cutter immediately while the fish is still warm.

Tips:

- Flying fish is traditionally deep-fried for this dish, but you can also grill or bake the fish fillets for a healthier option.
- Bajan seasoning can be found in Caribbean grocery stores or you can make your own blend using common spices.
- The sandwich rolls used for cutters are often crusty and substantial enough to hold the fillings without becoming soggy.

Enjoy your Barbadian Flying Fish Cutter, a delicious taste of Barbados that combines crispy fried fish with fresh vegetables and a kick of spice!

Jamaican Beef Patty

Dough Ingredients:

- 3 cups all-purpose flour
- 1 tsp turmeric (optional, for color)
- 1 tsp salt
- 1/2 cup cold unsalted butter, cut into small cubes
- 1/2 cup cold vegetable shortening (or lard), cut into small cubes
- 1/2 cup ice water, plus more as needed

Filling Ingredients:

- 1 lb ground beef
- 1 small onion, finely chopped
- 2 cloves garlic, minced
- 1/2 tsp dried thyme
- 1/2 tsp ground allspice
- 1/2 tsp curry powder
- 1/2 tsp paprika
- 1/4 tsp cayenne pepper (adjust to taste)
- Salt and pepper, to taste
- 1/2 cup beef broth or water
- 1/2 cup breadcrumbs
- 1/4 cup chopped fresh parsley (optional)

Egg Wash:

- 1 egg
- 1 tbsp water

Instructions:

1. **Make the dough:**
    - In a large bowl, whisk together the flour, turmeric (if using), and salt.
    - Add the cold butter and vegetable shortening (or lard) cubes. Use a pastry cutter or your fingers to blend the fats into the flour until the mixture resembles coarse crumbs.
    - Gradually add the ice water, 1 tablespoon at a time, mixing with a fork or your hands until the dough just comes together and forms a ball. Be careful not to overwork the dough.
    - Divide the dough into 8-10 equal portions, shape each portion into a ball, and flatten slightly into discs. Wrap each disc in plastic wrap and refrigerate for at least 30 minutes.

2. **Prepare the filling:**
   - In a large skillet or frying pan, cook the ground beef over medium heat until browned and cooked through, breaking it up with a spoon as it cooks.
   - Add the chopped onion, minced garlic, dried thyme, ground allspice, curry powder, paprika, cayenne pepper, salt, and pepper to the skillet. Cook for 2-3 minutes until the onions are softened and the spices are fragrant.
   - Stir in the beef broth (or water) and breadcrumbs. Cook for another 5-7 minutes, stirring occasionally, until the mixture is thickened and most of the liquid has evaporated.
   - Remove from heat and stir in chopped fresh parsley (if using). Let the filling cool completely before assembling the patties.
3. **Assemble the patties:**
   - Preheat your oven to 375°F (190°C). Line a baking sheet with parchment paper.
   - Take one dough disc at a time from the refrigerator. On a lightly floured surface, roll out each disc into a thin circle (about 1/8 inch thick).
   - Place a generous spoonful of the cooled beef filling onto one half of the dough circle, leaving a small border around the edges.
   - Fold the other half of the dough over the filling to form a half-moon shape. Press the edges firmly together with your fingers, then crimp the edges with a fork to seal. Repeat with the remaining dough discs and filling.
4. **Bake the patties:**
   - In a small bowl, whisk together the egg and water to make the egg wash.
   - Brush the tops of each patty with the egg wash.
   - Place the patties on the prepared baking sheet and bake for 25-30 minutes, or until the pastry is golden brown and cooked through.
5. **Serve:**
   - Remove from the oven and let the patties cool slightly before serving.
   - Enjoy your homemade Jamaican Beef Patties warm or at room temperature.

Tips:

- The turmeric is optional but adds a traditional golden color to the pastry.
- You can adjust the level of spiciness by varying the amount of cayenne pepper.
- Jamaican Beef Patties are often served with hot pepper sauce or ketchup on the side for dipping.

These Jamaican Beef Patties are perfect for a snack, lunch, or even as party appetizers. They are best enjoyed fresh out of the oven when the pastry is still crispy and the filling is savory and flavorful.

Trinidadian Corn Soup

Ingredients:

- 2 cups corn kernels (fresh or frozen)
- 1 lb chicken thighs, bone-in and skinless (optional)
- 1 onion, diced
- 3 cloves garlic, minced
- 1 carrot, diced
- 1 potato, diced
- 1 celery stalk, diced
- 1 bell pepper (any color), diced
- 1 scotch bonnet pepper, whole (optional, for heat)
- 1 can (14 oz) coconut milk
- 6 cups chicken or vegetable broth (or water)
- 1 tbsp fresh thyme leaves (or 1 tsp dried thyme)
- 1 tbsp fresh parsley, chopped
- 1 tbsp curry powder
- 1/2 tsp ground allspice
- Salt and pepper, to taste
- 2 tbsp vegetable oil

Instructions:

1. **Prepare the chicken (if using):**
   - Season the chicken thighs with salt and pepper.
   - In a large pot or Dutch oven, heat 1 tablespoon of vegetable oil over medium-high heat.
   - Brown the chicken thighs on both sides until golden brown, about 4-5 minutes per side. Remove the chicken and set aside.
2. **Make the soup base:**
   - In the same pot, add the remaining tablespoon of vegetable oil if needed.
   - Add the diced onion and sauté until translucent, about 3-4 minutes.
   - Stir in the minced garlic, curry powder, and ground allspice. Cook for another minute until fragrant.
3. **Simmer the soup:**
   - Return the chicken thighs to the pot (if using).
   - Add the diced carrot, potato, celery, bell pepper, and corn kernels.
   - Pour in the coconut milk and chicken or vegetable broth (or water).
   - Add the whole scotch bonnet pepper (if using) for flavor (do not slice unless you want more heat).
   - Stir in the fresh thyme leaves and parsley.
   - Season with salt and pepper to taste.
4. **Cook the soup:**

- Bring the soup to a boil, then reduce the heat to low. Cover and simmer for about 20-25 minutes, or until the vegetables are tender and the flavors have melded together.
- If using chicken thighs, remove them from the soup, shred the meat using two forks, and return the shredded chicken to the pot.

5. **Serve:**
    - Discard the scotch bonnet pepper before serving (if you do not want it to be too spicy).
    - Ladle the Trinidadian Corn Soup into bowls and serve hot.

Tips:

- Adjust the amount of scotch bonnet pepper based on your spice preference. Be cautious as it is very spicy.
- You can customize this soup by adding other vegetables like pumpkin or yam.
- Serve Trinidadian Corn Soup with a side of crusty bread or fried plantains for a complete meal.

Enjoy this Trinidadian Corn Soup, filled with Caribbean flavors and perfect for warming up on a chilly day or as a satisfying meal any time of year!

Antiguan Pepperpot

Ingredients:

- 1 lb stewing beef, cut into cubes
- 1 lb pork ribs, cut into pieces
- 1 lb oxtails (optional), cut into pieces
- 1 lb chicken pieces (legs or thighs)
- 1 lb smoked ham hock or smoked turkey wings (optional)
- 2 tbsp vegetable oil
- 1 large onion, chopped
- 4 cloves garlic, minced
- 2 bell peppers (any color), chopped
- 2 cups chopped okra
- 2 cups chopped spinach or callaloo leaves (substitute with kale or collard greens)
- 1 cup diced pumpkin or squash
- 1 cup diced yam or sweet potato
- 1 cup diced dasheen (taro) or cassava (yuca)
- 1-2 scotch bonnet peppers, whole (for flavor, remove before serving for less heat)
- 6 cups beef or chicken broth
- 1 cup coconut milk
- 2 tbsp tomato paste
- 1 tbsp ground allspice
- 1 tbsp ground cinnamon
- Salt and pepper, to taste
- Fresh thyme sprigs
- Fresh parsley or cilantro, chopped (for garnish)

Instructions:

1. **Prepare the meats:**
   - In a large pot or Dutch oven, heat the vegetable oil over medium-high heat.
   - Brown the stewing beef, pork ribs, oxtails (if using), chicken pieces, and smoked ham hock or turkey wings (if using) in batches until they are well-browned on all sides. Remove and set aside.
2. **Make the base:**
   - In the same pot, add more oil if needed. Sauté the chopped onion, garlic, and bell peppers until softened, about 5 minutes.
3. **Combine and simmer:**
   - Return the browned meats to the pot.
   - Stir in the chopped okra, spinach or callaloo leaves, diced pumpkin or squash, yam or sweet potato, and dasheen or cassava.
   - Add the scotch bonnet peppers (whole), beef or chicken broth, coconut milk, tomato paste, ground allspice, ground cinnamon, salt, and pepper.

- Tie the fresh thyme sprigs together with kitchen twine and add to the pot.
- Bring the mixture to a boil, then reduce the heat to low. Cover and simmer gently for 2 to 3 hours, stirring occasionally, until the meats are tender and the flavors have melded together. Add more broth if needed to keep the stew moist.

4. **Finish and serve:**
    - Discard the scotch bonnet peppers and thyme sprigs before serving.
    - Taste and adjust seasoning if needed.
    - Serve hot, garnished with chopped fresh parsley or cilantro.

Tips:

- Antiguan Pepperpot is traditionally served with bread or cornmeal dumplings.
- The longer the stew simmers, the richer the flavors will become. It's often made a day ahead and reheated for even better taste.
- Adjust the amount of scotch bonnet pepper according to your spice preference. Be cautious as it is very spicy.

Enjoy this hearty and comforting Antiguan Pepperpot, filled with a delicious blend of meats, vegetables, and aromatic spices that capture the essence of Caribbean cuisine!

Curry Conch

Ingredients:

- 1 lb conch meat, cleaned and tenderized (you can ask your fishmonger to tenderize it or use a meat mallet)
- 2 tbsp curry powder
- 1 onion, finely chopped
- 3 cloves garlic, minced
- 1-inch piece of ginger, minced
- 1 tomato, chopped
- 1 scotch bonnet pepper, whole (optional, for heat)
- 1 can (14 oz) coconut milk
- 1 cup seafood or chicken broth
- 2 tbsp vegetable oil
- 1 tbsp tomato paste
- Fresh cilantro or parsley, chopped (for garnish)
- Salt and pepper, to taste

Instructions:

1. **Prepare the conch:**
   - If the conch meat is not already tenderized, tenderize it by pounding gently with a meat mallet or rolling pin. Rinse thoroughly under cold water.
2. **Marinate the conch:**
   - In a bowl, mix the conch meat with 1 tablespoon of curry powder and a pinch of salt. Let it marinate for about 15-20 minutes.
3. **Cooking the curry:**
   - Heat the vegetable oil in a large pan or pot over medium heat.
   - Add the chopped onion and sauté until translucent, about 3-4 minutes.
   - Stir in the minced garlic and ginger, and cook for another 1-2 minutes until fragrant.
4. **Add the curry powder:**
   - Add the remaining tablespoon of curry powder and tomato paste. Stir well to combine and cook for another minute to toast the spices.
5. **Cook the conch:**
   - Add the marinated conch meat to the pan. Sauté for 2-3 minutes, stirring frequently, until the conch begins to turn opaque.
6. **Simmering:**
   - Pour in the coconut milk and seafood or chicken broth. Stir to combine.
   - Add the chopped tomato and whole scotch bonnet pepper (if using).
   - Season with salt and pepper to taste.

- Bring the mixture to a simmer, then reduce the heat to low. Cover the pan and let it simmer gently for about 15-20 minutes, or until the conch is tender and cooked through.
7. **Finish and serve:**
    - Once the conch is cooked through and the sauce has thickened slightly, remove the pan from heat.
    - Discard the scotch bonnet pepper (if used).
    - Garnish with chopped fresh cilantro or parsley.
    - Serve hot, either on its own or with rice or bread to soak up the flavorful curry sauce.

Tips:

- Adjust the amount of curry powder and scotch bonnet pepper according to your spice preference.
- Taste the curry before serving and adjust the seasoning with salt and pepper as needed.
- Conch can be tough if not tenderized properly, so ensure it's tender before serving.

Enjoy your homemade Curry Conch, a delightful dish that highlights the unique flavor and texture of conch with aromatic curry spices and creamy coconut milk!

Fish Amok (Caribbean-style)

Ingredients:

- 1 lb firm white fish fillets (such as snapper, grouper, or mahi-mahi), cut into bite-sized pieces
- 1 can (14 oz) coconut milk
- 1 small onion, finely chopped
- 3 cloves garlic, minced
- 1-inch piece of ginger, minced
- 1 tbsp curry powder
- 1 tsp ground turmeric
- 1 tsp ground cumin
- 1 tsp paprika
- 1 tbsp fish sauce
- 1 tbsp brown sugar (or palm sugar)
- Juice of 1 lime or lemon
- Salt and pepper, to taste
- Fresh cilantro or parsley, chopped (for garnish)
- Cooking oil

Instructions:

1. **Prepare the fish:**
   - Pat the fish fillets dry with paper towels. Season lightly with salt and pepper.
2. **Make the curry paste:**
   - In a small bowl, combine the minced garlic, minced ginger, curry powder, ground turmeric, ground cumin, and paprika. Add a splash of water to form a paste.
3. **Cooking the curry:**
   - Heat a tablespoon of cooking oil in a large skillet or wok over medium heat.
   - Add the chopped onion and sauté until translucent, about 3-4 minutes.
   - Add the curry paste to the skillet and cook for 1-2 minutes, stirring constantly, until fragrant.
4. **Add coconut milk and seasonings:**
   - Pour in the coconut milk, fish sauce, and brown sugar. Stir well to combine.
   - Bring the mixture to a simmer and cook for 5-7 minutes, stirring occasionally, to allow the flavors to meld together and the sauce to thicken slightly.
5. **Cook the fish:**
   - Gently add the fish pieces to the skillet, making sure they are submerged in the sauce.
   - Reduce the heat to low, cover the skillet, and let the fish simmer gently for about 8-10 minutes, or until the fish is cooked through and flakes easily with a fork.
6. **Finish and serve:**
   - Squeeze fresh lime or lemon juice over the fish.

- Taste and adjust seasoning with salt and pepper if needed.
- Garnish with chopped fresh cilantro or parsley.
- Serve hot over rice or with crusty bread to soak up the flavorful sauce.

Tips:

- You can add vegetables like bell peppers, zucchini, or spinach to the curry for added texture and nutrition.
- Adjust the amount of curry powder and spices according to your preference for heat and flavor.
- For a more traditional presentation, you can steam the fish in banana leaves or serve it in bowls with rice.

This Caribbean-style Fish Amok is a wonderful fusion of flavors, combining the richness of coconut milk with aromatic spices and the freshness of lime or lemon juice. It's a delightful dish that showcases the versatility of fish in Caribbean cuisine.

Barbadian Coo-coo

Ingredients:

- 1 cup cornmeal
- 2 cups water
- 1 cup coconut milk
- 1 small onion, finely chopped
- 1 small green bell pepper, finely chopped
- 1 small hot pepper (optional), finely chopped
- 2 cloves garlic, minced
- 1 tbsp butter or margarine
- Salt and black pepper, to taste

Instructions:

1. **Prepare the base:**
   - In a medium-sized saucepan, combine the water, coconut milk, chopped onion, bell pepper, hot pepper (if using), and garlic. Bring to a boil over medium-high heat.
2. **Add cornmeal:**
   - Gradually add the cornmeal to the boiling liquid, stirring continuously with a wooden spoon or whisk to prevent lumps from forming.
3. **Cook the coo-coo:**
   - Reduce the heat to low and continue to stir the mixture until it thickens and starts to pull away from the sides of the pan, similar to the consistency of mashed potatoes. This usually takes about 10-15 minutes.
   - Stir in the butter or margarine until melted and well incorporated.
   - Season with salt and black pepper to taste.
4. **Serve:**
   - Transfer the coo-coo to a serving dish and smooth the top with the back of a spoon.
   - Serve hot alongside your favorite fish dish, such as steamed or fried flying fish.

Tips:

- **Consistency:** The texture of coo-coo should be smooth and firm enough to slice, but not stiff.
- **Variations:** Some variations include adding okra for a thicker consistency or adding additional spices like thyme or bay leaves for extra flavor.
- **Presentation:** Traditionally, coo-coo is molded into a dome shape using a small bowl or mold before serving.

Barbadian Coo-coo is a comforting and versatile dish that complements the flavors of seafood dishes particularly well. It's not only delicious but also a wonderful way to experience the rich culinary heritage of Barbados.

Trinidadian Stewed Chicken

Ingredients:

- 1 whole chicken (about 3-4 lbs), cut into pieces
- 2 tbsp vegetable oil
- 1 onion, finely chopped
- 3 cloves garlic, minced
- 1 bell pepper (any color), diced
- 2 tomatoes, chopped
- 2 tbsp tomato paste
- 1 cup chicken broth or water
- 1 tsp dried thyme (or 1 tbsp fresh thyme leaves)
- 1 tsp paprika
- 1/2 tsp ground allspice
- 1/2 tsp ground cumin
- 1/2 tsp ground coriander
- 1/4 tsp cayenne pepper (adjust to taste)
- Salt and pepper, to taste
- Fresh cilantro or parsley, chopped (for garnish)

Instructions:

1. **Season and brown the chicken:**
    - Pat the chicken pieces dry with paper towels. Season generously with salt and pepper.
    - In a large, heavy-bottomed pot or Dutch oven, heat the vegetable oil over medium-high heat.
    - Brown the chicken pieces in batches until golden brown on all sides. Remove the chicken from the pot and set aside.
2. **Make the stew base:**
    - In the same pot, add a bit more oil if needed. Add the chopped onion and bell pepper. Sauté until softened, about 5 minutes.
    - Add the minced garlic and sauté for another minute until fragrant.
    - Stir in the chopped tomatoes and tomato paste. Cook for 3-4 minutes, stirring occasionally, until the tomatoes start to break down.
3. **Simmer the stew:**
    - Return the browned chicken pieces to the pot.
    - Add the chicken broth or water to the pot, along with dried thyme, paprika, ground allspice, ground cumin, ground coriander, and cayenne pepper.
    - Stir well to combine and bring the mixture to a simmer.
4. **Cook the chicken:**
    - Reduce the heat to low, cover the pot, and let the chicken simmer gently for 30-40 minutes, or until the chicken is cooked through and tender.

- Stir occasionally and add more broth or water if the sauce becomes too thick.
5. **Finish and serve:**
    - Taste and adjust seasoning with salt and pepper if needed.
    - Garnish with chopped fresh cilantro or parsley before serving.
    - Serve hot with rice, roti, or crusty bread to soak up the delicious stew sauce.

Tips:

- **Variations:** You can add diced potatoes, carrots, or other vegetables to the stew for added texture and flavor.
- **Spice Level:** Adjust the amount of cayenne pepper to suit your preference for spiciness.
- **Make Ahead:** This dish tastes even better the next day as the flavors have more time to meld together. Reheat gently on the stove or in the microwave.

Trinidadian Stewed Chicken is a comforting and satisfying dish that showcases the bold flavors of Caribbean spices and aromatics. It's perfect for a family meal or for entertaining guests, and it's sure to become a favorite in your kitchen!

Caribbean Seafood Paella

Ingredients:

- 1 lb shrimp, peeled and deveined
- 1 lb firm white fish fillets (such as snapper, mahi-mahi), cut into chunks
- 1 lb mussels and/or clams, cleaned and scrubbed
- 1 onion, finely chopped
- 3 cloves garlic, minced
- 1 bell pepper (any color), diced
- 1 scotch bonnet pepper, finely chopped (optional, adjust to taste)
- 1 cup chopped tomatoes
- 2 cups long-grain rice (such as jasmine or basmati)
- 4 cups seafood or chicken broth
- 1 cup coconut milk
- 1 tsp ground turmeric
- 1 tsp paprika
- 1 tsp ground cumin
- 1 tsp dried thyme (or 2 tsp fresh thyme leaves)
- Salt and pepper, to taste
- 2 tbsp vegetable oil
- Fresh cilantro or parsley, chopped (for garnish)
- Lemon or lime wedges, for serving

Instructions:

1. **Prepare the seafood:**
   - Season the shrimp and fish pieces with salt and pepper. Set aside.
2. **Sauté the aromatics:**
   - In a large paella pan or skillet, heat the vegetable oil over medium heat.
   - Add the chopped onion and bell pepper. Sauté for 3-4 minutes until softened.
3. **Add garlic and spices:**
   - Stir in the minced garlic, ground turmeric, paprika, ground cumin, and dried thyme. Cook for another minute until fragrant.
4. **Cook the rice:**
   - Add the chopped tomatoes to the pan. Cook for 3-4 minutes until the tomatoes start to break down.
   - Stir in the rice, coating it evenly with the onion and spice mixture.
5. **Add liquids:**
   - Pour in the seafood or chicken broth and coconut milk. Stir well to combine.
   - Bring the mixture to a simmer. Reduce the heat to medium-low and let it cook, uncovered, for about 15-20 minutes, or until the rice is almost tender and most of the liquid is absorbed. Stir occasionally.
6. **Add seafood:**

- Nestle the shrimp, fish chunks, and mussels/clams into the rice mixture. Arrange them evenly across the pan.
- Cover the pan and cook for another 5-7 minutes, or until the shrimp is pink and cooked through, the fish is opaque and flakes easily, and the mussels/clams have opened. Discard any mussels/clams that do not open.

7. **Finish and serve:**
   - Remove the pan from heat. Sprinkle chopped fresh cilantro or parsley over the paella.
   - Serve immediately with lemon or lime wedges on the side for squeezing over the paella.

Tips:

- **Variations:** Feel free to add other seafood like squid or scallops according to your preference.
- **Rice:** Ensure the rice is evenly distributed in the pan to cook evenly.
- **Spice Level:** Adjust the amount of scotch bonnet pepper according to your preference for heat.

Caribbean Seafood Paella is a vibrant and flavorful dish that brings together the best of Caribbean seafood with aromatic spices and creamy coconut milk. It's perfect for special occasions or as a hearty meal to enjoy with family and friends!

Grenadian Oil Down

Ingredients:

- 1 lb salted meat (salted pork, salted beef, or salted fish), soaked and cut into chunks
- 2 cups coconut milk
- 2 cups water
- 1 onion, sliced
- 2 cloves garlic, minced
- 1 bell pepper, sliced
- 2 carrots, sliced
- 1 cup diced pumpkin or squash
- 1 cup diced yam or sweet potato
- 1 cup diced dasheen (taro) or cassava (yuca)
- 2 cups spinach or callaloo leaves, chopped (substitute with kale or collard greens)
- 2 cups dumplings (recipe below)
- 2 tbsp vegetable oil
- Salt and pepper, to taste

Dumplings:

- 1 cup all-purpose flour
- 1/2 tsp salt
- Water, as needed

Instructions:

1. **Prepare the salted meat:**
   - If using salted meat, soak it in water overnight to remove excess salt. Cut into chunks before cooking.
2. **Make the dumplings:**
   - In a bowl, combine the flour and salt. Gradually add water and knead until a smooth dough forms. Roll into small balls or shape as desired.
3. **Cooking the Oil Down:**
   - In a large, heavy-bottomed pot or Dutch oven, heat the vegetable oil over medium heat.
   - Add the salted meat and sauté until lightly browned.
   - Add the sliced onion, minced garlic, and bell pepper. Sauté for a few minutes until softened and fragrant.
4. **Layering the ingredients:**
   - Add the coconut milk and water to the pot. Bring to a boil.
   - Add the diced pumpkin or squash, yam or sweet potato, dasheen or cassava, and dumplings.

- Reduce the heat to low and simmer gently, stirring occasionally, until the vegetables and dumplings are almost tender and most of the liquid has been absorbed. This may take about 30-40 minutes.

5. **Finish and serve:**
    - Stir in the chopped spinach or callaloo leaves. Cook for an additional 5-10 minutes until the greens are wilted and tender.
    - Taste and adjust seasoning with salt and pepper if needed.
    - Remove from heat and let it rest for a few minutes before serving.

Tips:

- **Variations:** Oil Down can include various vegetables depending on availability and personal preference. Some versions also include pieces of breadfruit.
- **Coconut Milk:** Freshly squeezed coconut milk is traditional and provides a rich, creamy texture. If using canned coconut milk, opt for full-fat for best results.
- **Dumplings:** You can shape the dumplings into balls or flatten them into discs before adding them to the pot.

Grenadian Oil Down is a comforting and satisfying dish that highlights the flavors of the Caribbean, with its rich coconut milk base and hearty vegetables. It's often enjoyed as a main course and is perfect for sharing with family and friends.

Bajan Cou-cou and Flying Fish

Ingredients:

- 1 cup cornmeal
- 2 cups water
- 1 cup okra, finely chopped
- 1 small onion, finely chopped
- 1 bell pepper, finely chopped
- 2 cloves garlic, minced
- 2 cups fish or vegetable broth
- 1 cup coconut milk
- 2 tbsp butter or margarine
- Salt and pepper, to taste

Instructions:

1. **Prepare the okra:**
   - In a bowl, mix the chopped okra with a pinch of salt and let it sit for about 10-15 minutes. This helps to reduce its sliminess.
2. **Cook the Cou-cou:**
   - In a heavy-bottomed pot, bring 2 cups of water to a boil.
   - Gradually add the cornmeal to the boiling water, stirring constantly with a whisk to prevent lumps.
   - Reduce the heat to low and continue stirring until the mixture thickens and pulls away from the sides of the pot, about 10-15 minutes.
3. **Add vegetables and seasonings:**
   - Stir in the chopped onion, bell pepper, and minced garlic. Cook for another 5 minutes, stirring frequently.
   - Gradually add the fish or vegetable broth, stirring constantly to combine.
   - Mix in the coconut milk and continue stirring until the mixture is smooth and creamy.
4. **Incorporate the okra:**
   - Add the salted okra to the cou-cou mixture. Stir well to combine.
   - Cook over low heat, stirring occasionally, for another 10-15 minutes until the okra is tender and the cou-cou has thickened to your desired consistency.
5. **Finish and serve:**
   - Stir in the butter or margarine until melted and well incorporated.
   - Taste and adjust seasoning with salt and pepper if needed.
   - Serve hot, alongside Flying Fish.

Flying Fish:

Ingredients:

- 4-6 whole flying fish (cleaned and scaled)
- 1 lemon, juiced
- Salt and pepper, to taste
- 2 tbsp vegetable oil or butter
- Fresh herbs (such as parsley or thyme), chopped (for garnish)

Instructions:

1. **Prepare the fish:**
   - Rinse the flying fish under cold water and pat dry with paper towels.
   - Rub the fish with lemon juice, salt, and pepper, ensuring it is evenly coated.
2. **Cook the fish:**
   - In a large skillet or frying pan, heat the vegetable oil or melt the butter over medium-high heat.
   - Place the flying fish in the skillet and cook for about 3-4 minutes on each side, or until golden brown and cooked through. The cooking time may vary depending on the thickness of the fish.
3. **Serve:**
   - Transfer the cooked flying fish to a serving platter.
   - Garnish with chopped fresh herbs, such as parsley or thyme.
   - Serve hot alongside Bajan Cou-cou.

Tips:

- **Okra:** If fresh okra is not available, you can use frozen okra. Thaw and chop it before adding it to the cou-cou.
- **Variations:** Some recipes include additional seasonings like thyme, bay leaves, or hot pepper sauce for extra flavor.
- **Presentation:** Traditionally, cou-cou is shaped into a dome before serving, often with a spoonful of sauce or gravy from the flying fish poured over the top.

Enjoy this delicious Bajan Cou-cou and Flying Fish, a true taste of Barbados that combines the creamy texture of cornmeal with the delicate flavor of flying fish, showcasing the island's rich culinary heritage.

Curry Crab

Ingredients:

- 2-3 lbs crab (cleaned and cracked, use fresh blue crab or any crab of your choice)
- 2 tbsp curry powder
- 1 onion, finely chopped
- 3 cloves garlic, minced
- 1-inch piece of ginger, minced
- 1 tomato, chopped
- 1 scotch bonnet pepper, whole (optional, for heat)
- 1 cup coconut milk
- 1 cup seafood or chicken broth
- 2 tbsp vegetable oil
- 1 tbsp tomato paste
- 1 tsp ground turmeric
- 1 tsp ground cumin
- 1 tsp ground coriander
- 1 tsp paprika
- Salt and pepper, to taste
- Fresh cilantro or parsley, chopped (for garnish)
- Lime wedges, for serving
- Cooked rice, for serving

Instructions:

1. **Prepare the crab:**
    - If the crab is whole, clean and crack it, removing the top shell and any gills. Rinse the crab pieces under cold water.
2. **Make the curry paste:**
    - In a small bowl, mix the curry powder, ground turmeric, ground cumin, ground coriander, and paprika with a splash of water to form a paste.
3. **Cooking the curry:**
    - In a large skillet or Dutch oven, heat the vegetable oil over medium heat.
    - Add the chopped onion and sauté until softened, about 3-4 minutes.
    - Stir in the minced garlic and ginger, and cook for another 1-2 minutes until fragrant.
4. **Add curry paste and tomatoes:**
    - Add the curry paste to the skillet. Stir well to combine and cook for 1-2 minutes to toast the spices.
    - Add the chopped tomato and tomato paste. Cook for another 3-4 minutes, stirring occasionally, until the tomatoes begin to break down.
5. **Simmer the crab:**

- Add the cleaned crab pieces to the skillet. Stir to coat them with the curry mixture.
- Pour in the coconut milk and seafood or chicken broth. Stir to combine.
- Add the whole scotch bonnet pepper (if using) for flavor, but keep it whole if you prefer less heat. Remember to remove it before serving if you don't want it to be spicy.
- Season with salt and pepper to taste.

6. **Cook until crab is done:**
   - Bring the mixture to a simmer. Reduce the heat to low, cover the skillet, and let it simmer gently for 15-20 minutes, or until the crab is cooked through and the sauce has thickened slightly.
   - Stir occasionally and adjust the seasoning if needed.
7. **Finish and serve:**
   - Discard the scotch bonnet pepper (if used).
   - Garnish with chopped fresh cilantro or parsley.
   - Serve hot with cooked rice and lime wedges on the side.

Tips:

- **Crab Preparation:** If using live crab, ensure it is cleaned thoroughly before cooking.
- **Spice Level:** Adjust the amount of scotch bonnet pepper or omit it entirely based on your preference for heat.
- **Variations:** You can add vegetables like bell peppers, carrots, or potatoes to the curry for added flavor and texture.

Curry Crab is a delightful dish that brings together the sweetness of crab meat with the aromatic spices of curry, creating a flavorful and satisfying meal. Enjoy this Caribbean favorite with friends and family, served over rice for a complete and delicious dining experience!

Jamaican Rice and Gungo Peas

Ingredients:

- 1 cup dried gungo peas (pigeon peas), soaked overnight (or canned gungo peas, drained and rinsed)
- 2 cups white rice (long-grain or jasmine)
- 1 small onion, finely chopped
- 2 cloves garlic, minced
- 1 scotch bonnet pepper, whole (optional, for flavor)
- 2 cups coconut milk
- 2 cups water (or chicken broth for added flavor)
- 2 tbsp vegetable oil
- 1 tsp dried thyme (or 1 tbsp fresh thyme leaves)
- 1 tsp ground allspice
- Salt and pepper, to taste
- Fresh cilantro or parsley, chopped (for garnish)

Instructions:

1. **Prepare the gungo peas:**
   - If using dried gungo peas, soak them overnight in water to soften. Drain and rinse before cooking.
2. **Sauté aromatics:**
   - In a large pot or Dutch oven, heat the vegetable oil over medium heat.
   - Add the chopped onion and sauté until softened, about 3-4 minutes.
   - Add the minced garlic and sauté for another minute until fragrant.
3. **Add rice and seasonings:**
   - Stir in the rice, thyme, and ground allspice. Coat the rice grains with the oil and aromatics, toasting them slightly for added flavor.
4. **Cook with coconut milk and water:**
   - Pour in the coconut milk and water (or chicken broth). Stir well to combine.
   - Add the soaked or canned gungo peas to the pot.
   - Add the whole scotch bonnet pepper (optional, for flavor). Keep it whole if you prefer less heat; remove it before serving if you don't want the dish to be spicy.
5. **Simmer and cook:**
   - Bring the mixture to a boil, then reduce the heat to low.
   - Cover the pot and let the rice simmer gently for 15-20 minutes, or until the rice is tender and all the liquid is absorbed. Avoid stirring the rice too often to prevent it from becoming sticky.
6. **Finish and serve:**
   - Once the rice is cooked, remove the pot from heat and discard the scotch bonnet pepper (if used).
   - Fluff the rice with a fork to separate the grains.

- Taste and adjust seasoning with salt and pepper if needed.
- Garnish with chopped fresh cilantro or parsley before serving.

Tips:

- **Variations:** You can add diced bell peppers, carrots, or diced tomatoes for additional flavor and color.
- **Spice Level:** Adjust the amount of scotch bonnet pepper according to your preference for heat.
- **Coconut Milk:** Use full-fat coconut milk for a richer and creamier texture.

Jamaican Rice and Gungo Peas is a flavorful and comforting dish that pairs well with a variety of Jamaican mains, such as jerk chicken or curry dishes. Enjoy this traditional recipe as a side or as a main dish for a taste of authentic Jamaican cuisine!

Caribbean Black Bean Soup

Ingredients:

- 2 cups dried black beans, soaked overnight (or 3 cans black beans, drained and rinsed)
- 2 tbsp olive oil or vegetable oil
- 1 onion, finely chopped
- 3 cloves garlic, minced
- 1 bell pepper (any color), diced
- 2 stalks celery, diced
- 1 carrot, diced
- 1 scotch bonnet pepper, whole (optional, for heat)
- 2 tsp ground cumin
- 1 tsp ground coriander
- 1 tsp paprika
- 1 tsp dried thyme (or 2 tsp fresh thyme leaves)
- 1 bay leaf
- 4 cups vegetable or chicken broth
- 1 cup coconut milk
- 1 tbsp tomato paste
- Juice of 1 lime or lemon
- Salt and pepper, to taste
- Fresh cilantro or parsley, chopped (for garnish)
- Sour cream or Greek yogurt (optional, for garnish)
- Sliced avocado (optional, for garnish)

Instructions:

1. **Prepare the beans:**
   - If using dried black beans, soak them overnight in water. Drain and rinse before cooking.
2. **Sauté aromatics:**
   - In a large pot or Dutch oven, heat the olive oil over medium heat.
   - Add the chopped onion, minced garlic, diced bell pepper, celery, and carrot. Sauté until the vegetables are softened, about 5-7 minutes.
3. **Add spices and herbs:**
   - Stir in the ground cumin, ground coriander, paprika, dried thyme, and bay leaf. Cook for another minute until fragrant.
4. **Cook the soup:**
   - Add the soaked or canned black beans to the pot.
   - Pour in the vegetable or chicken broth and coconut milk. Stir well to combine.
   - Add the whole scotch bonnet pepper (optional, for flavor). Keep it whole if you prefer less heat; remove it before serving if you don't want the soup to be spicy.
   - Stir in the tomato paste.

5. **Simmer and blend (optional):**
    - Bring the soup to a boil, then reduce the heat to low.
    - Cover and let the soup simmer gently for 1-1.5 hours, or until the beans are tender and flavors are well combined.
    - If desired, use an immersion blender to partially blend the soup for a smoother texture. Alternatively, blend a portion of the soup in a blender and return it to the pot.
6. **Finish and serve:**
    - Remove the scotch bonnet pepper (if used).
    - Stir in the lime or lemon juice.
    - Taste and adjust seasoning with salt and pepper if needed.
    - Ladle the soup into bowls and garnish with chopped fresh cilantro or parsley.
    - Optionally, top with a dollop of sour cream or Greek yogurt and sliced avocado.

Tips:

- **Variations:** Add diced potatoes, sweet potatoes, or spinach for added texture and nutrition.
- **Coconut Milk:** Use full-fat coconut milk for a richer and creamier soup.
- **Storage:** Caribbean Black Bean Soup can be stored in the refrigerator for up to 4 days or frozen for longer storage. Reheat gently on the stove or in the microwave before serving.

This Caribbean Black Bean Soup is not only delicious but also nutritious, packed with protein and fiber from the black beans and enriched with the flavors of coconut milk and Caribbean spices. Enjoy this comforting soup as a starter or a wholesome main course!

www.ingramcontent.com/pod-product-compliance
Lightning Source LLC
LaVergne TN
LVHW081602060526
838201LV00054B/2029